EXPL

THE

ABROAD OF

ITALY

Travel Guide

Floyd J. Ambrose

TABLE OF CONTENTS

-- -- -- -- -- -- -- -- -- -- --

INTRODUCTION

  - Welcome to Italy

  - Why Visit Italy?

  - How to Use This Guide

CHAPTER 1. Planning Your Trip

  - Best Time to Visit Italy

  - Visa Requirements

  - Currency and Money Matters

  - Transportation in Italy

  - Accommodation Options

CHAPTER 2. Essential Travel Information

- Italian Language and Basic Phrases

- Cultural Etiquette and Customs

- Safety Tips and Emergency Contacts

- Health and Medical Services

- Travel Insurance

CHAPTER 3. Exploring Italy: Top Destinations

- Rome

- Florence

- Venice

- Milan

- Naples

- Sicily

- Cinque Terre

- Amalfi Coast

- Tuscany

- The Italian Lakes

CHAPTER 4. Must-See Attractions and Landmarks

- Colosseum, Rome

- Vatican City

- Uffizi Gallery, Florence

- St. Mark's Square, Venice

- Duomo di Milano, Milan

- Pompeii

- Mount Vesuvius

- Capri Island

- Leaning Tower of Pisa

- Lake Como

CHAPTER 5. Experiencing Italian Cuisine

- Regional Italian Cuisine

- Popular Italian Dishes

- Wine and Food Pairings

- Dining Etiquette and Tips

- Cooking Classes and Food Tours

CHAPTER 6. Discovering Italian Culture

- Italian Art and Architecture

- Opera and Music

- Festivals and Celebrations

- Fashion and Shopping

- Sports and Recreation

CHAPTER 7. Outdoor Adventures in Italy

- Hiking in the Dolomites

- Cycling in Tuscany

- Water Sports along the Coast

- Skiing in the Italian Alps

- Sailing in the Mediterranean

CHAPTER 8. Traveling on a Budget

- Cost-Saving Tips

- Affordable Accommodation

- Cheap Eats and Local Markets

- Free Attractions and Activities

- Transportation Savings

CHAPTER 9. Language and Travel Resources

- Useful Italian Phrases

- Travel Apps and Websites

- Italian Cultural References

- Online Forums and Communities

CONCLUSION

- Final Tips and Recommendations

- Your Next Adventure Awaits!

BONUS: Quick Reference Guides

- Italian Phrases and Expressions

- Conversion Tables (Currency, Measurements)

- Emergency Contacts and Useful Numbers

INTRODUCTION

- WELCOME TO ITALY

Italy, situated in Southern Europe, is a compelling nation renowned for its rich history, breathtaking scenery, wonderful food, and cultural legacy. From the ancient ruins of Rome to the gorgeous canals of Venice, Italy provides a broad selection of experiences that will leave every traveler in wonder. So, let's begin on a tour to experience the attractions of this magnificent nation.

1. **History and Culture**: Italy has a remarkable history that extends over 2,000 years. It was the cradle of the Roman Empire, which had a lasting imprint on Western civilization. From the Colosseum and the Roman Forum in Rome to the beautifully maintained remains of Pompeii near Naples, history aficionados will find themselves immersed in the ancient world.

Italian culture is strongly established in history and is famed for its art, music, fashion, and architecture. Italy has been the home of great painters such as Leonardo da Vinci, Michelangelo, and Botticelli, whose works may be seen in museums and cathedrals around the nation. Opera also has a long-standing legacy in Italy, with major opera houses including La Scala in Milan and the Teatro San Carlo in Naples.

2. **Cities and Landmarks**: Italy provides a variety of renowned cities, each with its particular charm.

Rome, the Eternal City, is a must-visit location. Here, you may tour the Vatican City, home to St. Peter's Basilica and the Sistine Chapel, embellished with Michelangelo's stunning murals. The Roman Colosseum, the Pantheon, and the Trevi Fountain are some prominent monuments worth seeing in Rome.

Florence, the home of the Renaissance, is a paradise for art enthusiasts. The Uffizi Gallery holds an extraordinary collection of Renaissance art, including masterpieces by Botticelli, Raphael, and Titian. The beautiful Duomo, together with the neighboring Baptistery and Bell Tower, dominates the city's skyline.

Venice, the City of Canals, is a unique and charming location. Take a gondola ride along the meandering canals, see St. Mark's Square and the Doge's Palace, and explore the picturesque towns of Burano and Murano, noted for their lace and glass-making traditions.

Other notable cities include Milan, a fashion and design capital, with its grand Gothic cathedral (Duomo) and world-class shopping; Naples, known for its vibrant street life, historic center, and proximity to the archaeological sites of Pompeii and Herculaneum; and the cliffside towns of the Amalfi Coast, such as Positano and Ravello, offering breathtaking views of the Mediterranean Sea.

3. **Cuisine and Wine**: Italian cuisine is famous internationally for its simplicity, fresh ingredients, and wonderful taste. Each area has its culinary specialties, such as pasta dishes from Bologna, pizza from Naples, and risotto from Milan. Indulge in delectable gelato, real Neapolitan pizza, and classic meals like spaghetti carbonara, lasagna, and ossobuco.

Italy is also a wine lover's heaven, producing some of the world's greatest wines. From Tuscany's Chianti to Piedmont's Barolo, the nation provides a vast choice of varieties to satisfy every taste. Consider visiting the vineyards of the Valpolicella area near Verona or exploring the wine roads of Tuscany and Umbria.

4. **Natural Beauty**: Italy's landscapes are tremendously varied, ranging from the snow-capped heights of the Italian Alps to the sun-soaked beaches of Sicily. The nation is home to gorgeous lakes like Lake Como and Lake Garda, surrounded by attractive villages and villas. The Dolomites in northern Italy provide a spectacular landscape, making them a paradise for outdoor lovers and photographers alike. With its rugged peaks, lush meadows, and unambiguous lakes, the Dolomites provide spectacular vistas and infinite chances for hiking, skiing, and rock climbing.

Italy's shores are similarly gorgeous. The Amalfi Coast entices travelers with its majestic cliffs, colorful fishing towns, and turquoise seas. Sardinia features beautiful beaches and turquoise bays, while the rugged beauty of Cinque Terre's coastal settlements makes a lasting impact. Whether you desire mountains or the sea, Italy's natural beauty will capture your heart.

In conclusion, Italy draws tourists with its seductive combination of history, art, gastronomy, and natural marvels. The country's cultural treasures, from prehistoric ruins to Renaissance masterpieces, leave visitors in awe of human effort over the years. The various landscapes, from the magnificent Alps to the sun-drenched coasts and calm lakes, offer a playground for outdoor lovers and a source of inspiration for painters and photographers. Moreover, the enticing tastes of Italian food, complemented by outstanding wines, delight even the most discriminating palates.

Whether you're wandering through the streets of Rome, enjoying the art in Florence, sailing through the canals of Venice, or reveling in the seaside grandeur of the Amalfi Coast, Italy delivers a sensory feast that remains long after your stay. The warmth and openness of the Italian people lend an added layer of appeal to the experience, making you feel welcome and welcomed by the country's cultural tapestry.

In Italy, you may immerse yourself in history, experience delicious cuisines, discover natural marvels, and make treasured memories. Each area has its character and riches to uncover, guaranteeing that every journey to Italy is unique and enjoyable.

So, whether you're an art enthusiast, a history buff, a culinary lover, or just wishing to bask in the beauty of nature, Italy welcomes you to embark on a journey of discovery, enchantment, and sheer joy. Come and experience the enchantment of Italy for yourself, and let it leave an unforgettable impact on your heart and spirit.

- Why Visit Italy?

Italy, with its rich history, lively culture, and magnificent scenery, ranks as one of the most tempting places in the world. From ancient ruins and architectural wonders to excellent art, delectable food, and stunning beaches, Italy provides a riveting experience for tourists of all interests. This thorough book will dig into the reasons why Italy should be at the top of your trip list, examining the country's historical riches, cultural legacy, natural marvels, and gastronomic pleasures.

1. **Historical and Cultural Marvels**: Italy's historical history is unsurpassed, with vestiges of ancient civilizations and creative treasures spanning thousands of years. Rome, the Eternal City, beckons with renowned structures such as the Colosseum, Roman Forum, and the Vatican City, where St. Peter's Basilica and the Sistine Chapel capture tourists with their ageless beauty. The ancient remains of Pompeii and

Herculaneum give a fascinating view into Roman life trapped in time by the explosion of Mount Vesuvius.

Florence, the home of the Renaissance, features architectural masterpieces such as the Florence Cathedral (Duomo), the Uffizi Gallery, and Michelangelo's David. Venice, with its lovely canals and stately palaces, generates a feeling of romance and mystery. Throughout the region, you'll encounter magnificent medieval cities, such as Siena, San Gimignano, and Assisi, whose narrow cobblestone alleyways and old structures transport you to a bygone age.

2. **Artistic Masterpieces**: Italy's contribution to the world of art is enormous, with great painters like Leonardo da Vinci, Michelangelo, and Botticelli calling this nation home. Museums and galleries highlight these masterpieces, including the eternal beauty of da Vinci's The Last Supper in Milan, Michelangelo's renowned statues in Florence's Accademia Gallery, and Botticelli's Birth of Venus in the Uffizi Gallery.

Venice's Biennale art show, held every two years, draws art fans from across the world, while the dynamic street art movement in Rome and Milan gives a modern touch on Italy's creative past. Whether you're an art expert or just admire beauty, Italy's art culture will leave you inspired and awe-struck.

3. **Breathtaking Natural Landscapes**: Italy's numerous landscapes are a monument to its natural beauty. From the snow-capped summits of the Italian Alps to the sun-drenched beaches of the Amalfi Coast, Italy provides a feast for the eyes. The Dolomites, a UNESCO World Heritage site, has spectacular mountain ranges, crystal-clear lakes, and charming alpine settlements, drawing hikers, climbers, and nature lovers.

The Amalfi Coast, with its rocky cliffs, blue waves, and colorful towns clinging to the hillsides, is a Mediterranean paradise. The undulating hills of Tuscany, filled with vineyards and olive groves, give postcard-perfect beauty. Italy's islands, including Sicily, Sardinia, and Capri, offer gorgeous beaches, crystal-clear oceans, and distinct cultural experiences.

4. **Culinary Delights**: Italian food is known internationally for its simplicity, fresh ingredients, and robust tastes. Each area in Italy has its culinary peculiarities and traditions, delivering a distinct gourmet experience.

Indulge in scrumptious pasta dishes like carbonara, amatriciana, and pesto; experience real Neapolitan pizza in its home, Naples; and savor the aromas of regional cuisines like risotto in Lombardy or bistecca alla fiorentina in Tuscany.

Italy's gastronomic joys extend beyond pasta and pizza. Sample artisanal cheeses like Parmigiano-Reggiano, mozzarella, and gorgonzola, combined with classic cured meats like prosciutto and salami. Indulge in the delicious tastes of risotto, osso buco, and tiramisu. And let's not forget the world of gelato, where you may indulge your taste buds in a diversity of flavors, from traditional pistachio and stracciatella to new combinations like fig and balsamic vinegar.

5. **Warm welcome & Cultural Immersion**: Italians are famous for their warm welcome and love for life. When you visit Italy, you'll be greeted by the friendly inhabitants who take delight in sharing their culture and customs. Whether you're wandering through crowded markets, joining in on a colorful festival, or just having a discussion over a cup of espresso at a local café, you'll experience a feeling of

belonging and a chance to immerse yourself in the Italian way of life.

6. **Diverse Experiences for Every Traveler**: Italy caters to a broad variety of interests, making it a perfect destination for all sorts of tourists. History aficionados may visit ancient ruins, medieval castles, and Renaissance palaces. Outdoor enthusiasts may trek through national parks, ski in the Alps, or sail along the magnificent coasts. Art aficionados may appreciate treasures in outstanding museums and galleries. Food connoisseurs may go on culinary excursions, wine tastings, and cooking workshops. And for those seeking leisure, Italy offers stunning beaches, lovely rural getaways, and exquisite spa treatments.

In conclusion, Italy's attractiveness rests in its seamless combination of history, culture, natural beauty, and gourmet pleasures. From the renowned sights of Rome to the serene beauty of Tuscany, Italy provides a multifaceted experience that makes a lasting effect on every visitor. Whether you're discovering ancient ruins, indulging in exquisite food, immersing yourself in art and culture, or just soaking in the grandeur of the country's landscapes, Italy offers a trip full of enchantment, discovery, and memorable experiences.

- How to Use This Guide

Welcome to Exploring the Abroad of Italy! This thorough travel guide is intended to help you make your way through the delights of this enchanting nation in 2023 and beyond. Whether you're a first-time visitor or want to explore Italy in greater detail, this book will give you critical information, practical ideas, and insightful suggestions to make the most of your Italian journey.

1. **Introduction to Italy**: Start by acquainting yourself with Italy's geography, history, and cultural attractions. Learn about the diverse regions, prominent cities, and renowned attractions that make Italy a must-visit trip. Understanding the country's variety and rich legacy will improve your entire vacation experience.

2. **Organizing Your Trip**: Begin your adventure by organizing your itinerary. Determine the period of your trip, pick the areas and cities you intend to visit, and explain your travel preferences. This book will offer you an

overview of Italy's greatest attractions, enabling you to construct a well-rounded itinerary that meets your interests and timetable.

3. **Essential Travel Information**: Gather practical information to facilitate smooth travel. Learn about admission criteria, visa laws, currency exchange, and transit choices inside Italy. This section will give you vital insights on the best time to visit Italy, weather conditions, and local traditions to help you prepare for your vacation.

4. **Exploring Italy's Top Destinations**: Discover the highlights of Italy's most renowned cities, such as Rome, Florence, Venice, Milan, and Naples. Each city has its particular appeal and attractions, including historic sites, world-renowned museums, art galleries, and gastronomic pleasures. This book will give insights into must-see landmarks, off-the-beaten-path activities, and local suggestions to enrich your visit to each region.

5. **Embracing Italian Culture**: Immerse yourself in Italy's rich cultural legacy by discovering its art, architecture, and rituals. Learn about the Renaissance masterpieces, see prominent museums and galleries, and experience the thriving cultural environment

that penetrates every part of the nation. This section will lead you through Italy's cultural riches and help you understand its creative past.

6. **Indulging in Italian food**: One of Italy's greatest joys is its food. Delight in the tastes of real Italian meals, from pasta and pizza to regional specialties and gelato. This book will expose you to traditional recipes, highlight local food markets, propose preferred eateries, and give insights into the art of combining food with area wines. Get ready to go on a culinary tour across Italy's gastronomic wonders.

7. **Practical ideas and guidance**: Make the most of your vacation with practical ideas and guidance. Learn about local transportation alternatives, navigating public transit systems, and locating lodgings that fit your budget. Discover how to be safe and healthy during your travels and educate yourself about Italian etiquette and traditions. This section will provide you with the information to traverse Italy with confidence and comfort.

8. **Extra Resources**: Enhance your vacation experience by exploring extra resources that go further into Italy's history, culture, and attractions. This guide will propose books, films, music, and other sources that give

essential insights and more inspiration for your trip.

In conclusion, Italy awaits its magnificent history, beautiful scenery, rich culture, and exquisite food. This travel guide is your key to uncovering the beauty and charm of Italy in 2023 and beyond. Use this book as your companion to organize your schedule, explore the country's attractions, and immerse yourself in the Italian way of life. Embrace the romance of Italy as you make unique experiences and go on a trip that will have you wishing to return. Buon Viaggio! (Have a good vacation!)

CHAPTER 1. Planning Your Trip

- Best Time to Visit Italy

Italy is a country that provides various experiences throughout the year, making it a terrific location to visit at any time. However, the ideal time to visit Italy depends on your interests, the activities you want to participate in, and the locations you desire to discover. Here's an overview of the seasons and what they offer:

1. **Spring (April to June)**: Spring is one of the most popular months to visit Italy. The weather is often moderate and pleasant, with blossoming flowers and rich sceneries. It's a wonderful season for seeing cities, visiting historical sites, and enjoying outdoor sports. The crowds are lower compared to the busy summer season, providing for a more leisurely vacation experience. You may also witness cultural events and festivals during this season, such as the Infiorata flower festival in Spello or the famed Palio horse race in Siena.

2. **Summer (June to August):** Summer in Italy is known for bright festivals, busy beach resorts, and outdoor eating. The weather is hot and bright, particularly in the southern regions and coastal districts. It's a terrific time for sun-seekers and beach fans. Popular places like Rome, Florence, and Venice might become busy around this period, but you continue to locate tranquil areas in smaller towns and off-the-beaten-path locales. If you want to visit major tourist destinations, it's better to reserve tickets in advance to avoid excessive lineups.

3. **Fall (September to October):** Fall is another good season to visit Italy, with nice temperatures and magnificent fall colors. The crowds start to thin out, giving it a great time for touring cities, museums, and art galleries without the peak-season congestion. The area is especially gorgeous this season, with vineyards and olive orchards in full harvest mode. It's a perfect time for wine tasting and visiting the famed truffle festivals in locations like Piedmont and Umbria. The seaside districts also maintain their attractiveness, with warmer temperatures and fewer visitors.

4. **Winter (November to February)**: Winter in Italy is a magnificent period, particularly in locations like the Dolomites and Alps, where you can enjoy skiing and winter sports. The cities are decked with festive decorations, and there's a warm mood in the air. It's a wonderful time to tour cultural monuments, and museums, and enjoy Italy's gastronomic pleasures. The winter season gives the benefit of fewer people and reduced accommodation charges, except around the Christmas and New Year vacations. However, it's crucial to know that certain attractions and tourist sites may have restricted hours or closures during this season.

It's worth remembering that Italy's climate differs drastically from north to south. The northern parts have colder winters, whereas the south gets warmer weather. If you're planning outdoor activities like hiking or visiting the Amalfi Coast, it's essential to verify the exact weather conditions for those places.

Ultimately, the ideal time to visit Italy depends on your interests and tastes. Consider the activities you wish to indulge in, the amount of crowd tolerance, and the weather conditions that fit with your ideal trip experience.

- Visa Requirements

Italy, recognized for its rich history, art, and stunning scenery, is a favorite destination for visitors from across the globe. If you are considering a trip to Italy, it's necessary to educate yourself about the visa requirements to guarantee a smooth and simple voyage. In this article, we will present detailed information regarding visa requirements for Italy.

Visa Exemptions: Italy is a part of the Schengen Area, which provides for the free movement of persons within its member nations. Citizens of certain countries are free from acquiring a visa for Italy if their stay is for tourism, business, or family visits for up to 90 days within 180 days. The following are some of the nations whose citizens enjoy visa exemptions:

1. **European Union (EU) and European Free Trade Association (EFTA) countries**: Citizens of EU and EFTA countries, including Austria, Belgium, Denmark, Finland, France, Germany, Iceland, Liechtenstein, Luxembourg, Netherlands, Norway, Portugal, Spain, Sweden,

and Switzerland, do not require a visa to enter Italy.

2. **Non-EU countries with visa exemptions**: Citizens of various countries, including the United States, Canada, Australia, New Zealand, Japan, South Korea, and many more, are free from acquiring a visa for Italy for short-term stays.

It's vital to know that visa exemptions may have various limits and requirements. For example, the aim of the visit should be tourism, business, or family visits, and the period of stay should not exceed 90 days within 180 days.

3. **Schengen Visa**: If you are a citizen of a country not included in the visa exemption list or if you want to remain in Italy for more than 90 days, you will need to apply for a Schengen visa. The Schengen visa is a short-stay visa that permits you to travel to and remain in Italy and other Schengen Area countries for up to 90 days within 180 days.

Here are the processes to apply for a Schengen visa for Italy:

1. **choose the kind of visa**: Depending on the purpose of your visit, you need to choose a suitable visa type. The most prevalent

categories are tourist visas, business visas, and guest visas for family or friends.

2. **Find the relevant embassy or consulate**: Contact the Italian embassy or consulate in your home country to receive the essential application paperwork and information about the application procedure. You may also need to book an appointment for submitting your application.

3. **Gather the required documents**: Prepare all the required documents for your visa application, which may include a valid passport, completed use form, recent passport-sized photographs, an example for trip insurance, travel itinerary, lodging bookings, evidence of financial means, and any supporting documents based on the purpose of your visit.

4. **Apply**: Visit the embassy or consulate in person on the arranged appointment day to submit your application. Pay the appropriate visa cost at this time as well.

5. **Attend the visa interview**: In certain situations, you may be asked to attend a visa interview. Be prepared to answer inquiries about your trip plans, the reason for the visit, and your financial position.

6. **Wait for the decision**: The processing period for a Schengen visa might vary, but it normally takes roughly 15 calendar days. During this period, the embassy or consulate will analyze your application and make a decision. It's advisable to apply well in advance of your scheduled trip dates to allow for any unanticipated delays.

7. **Collect your visa**: If your visa application is granted, you may collect your passport with the visa at the embassy or consulate. Make careful to verify the visa information for correctness before leaving the premises.

Additional Information:

1. **Long-stay visas**: If you want to remain in Italy for more than 90 days, you will need to apply for a long-stay visa, which is referred to as a national passport or a Type D visa. Long-stay visas are frequently issued for objectives such as job, study, family reunion, or residency. The application procedure and conditions for long-stay visas are different from short-stay European visas.

2. **Visa extensions**: If you are currently in Italy and need to extend your stay beyond the 90-day restriction, you should contact the local

Questura (Police Headquarters) before your visa expires. They will give you the relevant information and help you through the extension procedure.

3. **Residency permits**: If you want to remain in Italy for any lengthy term, you may want to apply for a residency permit (permesso di soggiorno) after arriving in the country. Residence permits are necessary for foreign citizens residing in Italy for longer than 90 days.

It's vital to note that visa requirements might vary over time, so it's best to check with the Italian embassy or consulate in your country or the Ministry of Foreign Affairs website for the most up-to-date and correct information on visa requirements for Italy.

- Currency and Money Matters

When planning a vacation to Italy, it's vital to comprehend the country's currency and have a thorough understanding of money-related concerns. This thorough guide will offer you crucial information on currency, banking, exchanging money, and utilizing payment methods in Italy.

Currency: The official currency of Italy is the Euro (€). It is the generally recognized method of payment in the nation. The Euro is split into 100 cents, with coins available in denominations of 1, 2, 5, 10, 20, and 50 cents, as well as 1 and 2 Euro coins. Banknotes exist in denominations of 5, 10, 20, 50, 100, 200, and 500 Euros.

Exchanging Money:

To get Euros for your trip to Italy, you have various options:

1. **Currency convert**: You may convert your native currency for Euros at banks, post offices, currency exchange offices, or approved conversion kiosks. Banks normally provide reasonable rates, although they may demand greater charges or fees. It's recommended to examine rates and costs before completing the trade.

2. **ATMs**: Italy has a large network of ATMs (Automatic Teller Machines) where you may withdraw cash using your debit or credit card. ATMs usually give competitive exchange rates. However, be cautious of any costs that your home bank or card issuer may incur for foreign withdrawals.

Credit Cards and Debit Cards: Credit and debit cards are readily accepted at all places in Italy, including hotels, restaurants, stores, and tourist attractions. Major credit cards such as Visa, Mastercard, and American Express are routinely accepted. However, it's a good idea to carry some cash, particularly for tiny enterprises or in rural places where card acceptance may be restricted.

Before your vacation, contact your bank or card issuer about your travel intentions to prevent any possible complications with your cards being stopped due to suspected fraudulent activity.

3. Traveler's Checks: Traveler's checks have grown less common in recent years, and their acceptability in Italy may be restricted. It might be tough to discover locations that take traveler's checks, therefore it's advisable to depend on alternative payment options such as cash or cards.

4. **Tipping and Service Costs**: In Italy, service costs are generally included in the bill at restaurants and cafés. However, it's common to round up the amount or give a tiny extra tip as a

token of gratitude for outstanding service. Tipping is not mandatory but is considered a courteous gesture. If you experience great service, you may opt to give a slightly bigger tip.

5. **Safety & Security:** Italy, like any other location, has its share of pickpocketing and theft concerns, particularly in popular tourist areas. Here are some measures to secure the safety of your money:

1. Carry just the cash you need for the day and store it in a safe area, such as a money belt or a concealed bag.

2. Use ATMs situated in well-lit and safe settings, such as within banks or retail malls.

3. Be careful while using your cards in public locations and conceal the PIN each time you use them.

4. Keep a photocopy or digital scan of your passport, credit card, and other critical papers in case of loss or theft.

6. **Banking Hours**: Banking hours in Italy are normally from Monday to Friday, from 8:30 am to 1:30 pm, with some banks reopening for a few hours in the afternoon. It's essential to remember that banking hours may vary, particularly in smaller towns or during holidays,

so it's recommended to verify the precise hours of the bank you want to visit.

In conclusion, familiarizing yourself with the currency, payment methods, and money-related problems in Italy can assist you to navigate the financial environment with ease and make your transactions seamless and hassle-free."

- Transportation in Italy

Italy is famous for its rich history, magnificent scenery, and dynamic cities, and traveling about this lovely nation is made easier owing to its excellent transit network. Whether you're touring ancient ruins, busy cities, or gorgeous countryside, Italy provides a range of transportation alternatives to fit any traveler's demands. From trains and buses to vehicles and ferries, here's a full guide to transportation in Italy.

1. **Trains**: Italy has an enormous railway system that is often recognized as one of the finest in Europe. Trenitalia is a national railway business that runs both regional and high-speed trains. The high-speed trains, known as Frecciarossa, Frecciargento, and Frecciabianca, link major cities including Rome, Milan, Florence, Venice,

and Naples with astonishing speed and comfort. It's essential to buy your tickets in advance, particularly during high travel seasons, to obtain the greatest rates and seating possibilities.

2. **Buses**: Buses are a cheap and convenient method to move within and between cities in Italy. The largest bus operator, owned by Trenitalia, is named FlixBus, giving links to several places around the country. Additionally, many cities have bus systems, which are a fantastic choice for touring inside city borders. However, bear in mind that bus travel may be slower than trains, especially for larger distances.

3. **Metro and Trams**: Major cities in Italy, such as Rome, Milan, Naples, Turin, and Palermo, have efficient metro systems that offer a speedy and dependable form of transit throughout the metropolitan regions. These metros are especially handy for traveling through city cores and visiting famous tourist destinations. Additionally, trams are accessible in various cities, giving another simple method to travel about.

4. **Rental Cars**: If you prefer the freedom of driving on your own, renting a vehicle in Italy is a reasonable alternative. However, it's vital to

realize that driving in Italian cities may be tough owing to excessive traffic and few parking spots. Renting a vehicle is best suited for touring the countryside or less heavily inhabited places. Remember to educate yourself about the local traffic rules and get an International Driving Permit if applicable.

5. **Ferries**: With Italy's vast coastline and many islands, ferries play a key role in transportation. The most notable ferry lines link mainland Italy with Sardinia, Sicily, and the Aeolian Islands. Ferry services provide a picturesque and delightful method to visit these sites, enabling you to admire the grandeur of the Mediterranean Sea.

6. **Air Travel**: For long-distance travel or if you're short on time, domestic flights inside Italy might be a practical alternative. Several airlines run domestic flights, giving connections between major cities and famous tourist attractions. However, it's worth remembering that airports are generally situated outside the city cores, which may demand extra travel time and expenditures to reach your ultimate destination.

7. **Taxis and Ridesharing**: Taxis are easily accessible in most Italian cities, and they may be called on the street or located at authorized taxi stops. Make sure the taxi is legitimate, with a meter and license shown. Ridesharing services like Uber are also accessible in major cities, giving an alternative to regular taxis.

In conclusion, Italy provides a varied choice of transportation alternatives that accommodate different interests and budgets. Whether you choose to travel by rail, bus, car, boat, or aircraft, planning your trips will assist guarantee easy and effective travel around this interesting nation. Remember to consider aspects like cost, convenience, and the unique demands of your schedule to select the most acceptable transportation options throughout your stay in Italy.

- Accommodation Options

Italy is a renowned tourist destination recognized for its rich history, lively culture, breathtaking scenery, and wonderful food. Whether you're planning a romantic break, a family vacation, or a solitary excursion, selecting the correct hotel is vital for a pleasant and comfortable stay. Italy provides a broad selection of hotel alternatives to suit every budget, taste, and desire. From expensive hotels to warm bed & breakfasts, lovely villas, and affordable hostels, here are some extensive data regarding housing alternatives in Italy.

1. **Hotels**: Italy provides a broad range of hotels, ranging from opulent 5-star places to more inexpensive 3-star ones. Major cities like Rome, Florence, Venice, and Milan offer a vast choice of hotels catering to diverse budgets and interests. Luxury hotels frequently have attractive décor, excellent facilities, local restaurants, spas, and concierge services. Mid-range hotels offer pleasant rooms with needed facilities, while budget hotels give economical but adequate lodgings.

2. **Bed and Breakfasts (B&Bs)**: Italy is famed for its attractive bed and breakfasts, especially in smaller towns and rural regions. B&Bs provide a more customized and intimate experience, with pleasant hosts typically giving handmade meals and local insights. These lodgings often feature a restricted number of rooms, providing a pleasant and homey feel. B&Bs are a terrific alternative for those wanting

a more genuine and immersive Italian experience.

3. **Agriturismo**: For a unique rural experience, consider vacationing in an agriturismo. These lodgings are mainly functioning farms or rural estates that provide guest rooms or flats. Agriturismos enable guests to immerse themselves in the agricultural culture of Italy, including activities like wine tasting, olive oil manufacturing, and farm-to-table eating. This choice is great for people wishing to unwind in a calm atmosphere and enjoy the picturesque countryside.

4. **Villas and Apartments**: Renting a villa or apartment may be an ideal alternative for families, parties, or anyone planning an extended trip to Italy. Villas are often bigger, separate residences with gardens, pools, and adequate room for leisure and entertainment. Apartments, on the other hand, are frequently placed inside residential buildings and provide a more local feel. Many companies and businesses specialize in holiday rentals, giving a large range of residences around Italy.

5. **Hostels**: Ideal for budget-conscious visitors and backpackers, hostels provide economical housing with shared amenities such as

dormitory-style rooms, community kitchens, and common spaces. Italy has several hostels, notably in renowned tourist locations and large towns. Staying in hostels not only helps save money but also gives possibilities to meet other travelers and participate in social events.

6. **Boutique Hotels**: Italy is recognized for its beautiful and distinctive boutique hotels, which frequently contain modern design features, creative flair, and customized services. Boutique hotels provide a more personal and customized experience, with attention to detail and individualized customer care. These hotels are great for guests seeking a combination of luxury, elegance, and character.

7. **Monasteries & Convents**: For a genuinely unusual and eccentric experience, try staying in a monastery or convent. Many religious houses in Italy welcome guests and provide simple but acceptable lodgings. These calm getaways frequently offer historic buildings, beautiful grounds, and a relaxing ambiance. Staying at a monastery or convent may give a feeling of spirituality and a reprieve from the rush and bustle of tourist regions.

When arranging your lodging in Italy, consider variables such as location, price, facilities, and the sort of experience you seek. It's essential to reserve early, particularly during busy tourist seasons, to guarantee the greatest alternatives and costs. Additionally, reading reviews and comparing costs on credible travel websites will help you make an educated selection.

Whether you select a posh hotel, a nice bed, and breakfast, a rustic agriturismo, or any other lodging choice, Italy's unique offers are guaranteed to deliver a memorable and delightful stay.

CHAPTER 2. Essential Travel Information

- Italian Language and Basic Phrases

Italian is a Romance language spoken by about 85 million people globally. It is the official language of Italy, San Marino, Switzerland (Ticino and Graubünden cantons), Vatican City, and the European Union. Additionally, it is extensively spoken in locations such as southern Switzerland, Monaco, Malta, Croatia, Slovenia, and many groups across the globe having Italian origin.

The Italian language has a rich cultural and historical legacy, and learning even a few simple words will substantially enrich your experience while visiting Italy or engaging with Italian people. Here are some fundamental Italian words to help you get started:

Greetings and Basic Expressions:

1. Ciao! - Hello!/Goodbye!
2. Buongiorno! - Good morning!
3. Buonasera! - Good evening!
4. Buonanotte! - Good night!
5. Come stai? - How are you?

6. Mi chiamo [your name]. - My name is [your name].

7. Piacere! - Nice to meet you!

8. Grazie! - Thank you!

9. Prego! - You're welcome!

10. Scusa/Scusami! - Excuse me!

11. Mi dispiace. - I'm sorry.

Common Courtesies:

12. Per favor! - Please!

13. Perdono! - Pardon me!

14. Mi può aiutare? - Can you assist me?

15. Parla inglese? - Do you speak English?

16. Non-Capisco. - I don't understand.

17. Può ripetere, per favore? - Can you repeat, please?

18. Mi potrebbe dare indicazioni per...? - Could you offer me instructions to...?

19. Mi può consigliere un buon ristorante? - Can you suggest a decent restaurant?

20. A che ora chiude/are? - What time does it close/open?

Numbers and Counting:

21. Uno, due, tre, quattro, cinque - One, two, three, four, five

22. Dieci, venti, trenta, Quaranta, cinquanta - Ten, twenty, thirty, forty, fifty

23. Cento, mille - One hundred, one thousand

24. Quanto Costa? - How much does it cost?

25. Vorrei... - I would want...

Eating and Ordering:

26. Un tavolo per uno/due, per favore. - A table for one/two, please.

27. Posso avere il menù? - Can I get the menu?

28. Vorrei ordinary... - I would like to order...

29. Mi può consigliere un piatto tipico? - Can you suggest a typical dish?

30. Il conto, per favore. - The bill, please.

Getting Around:

31. Dove si trova...? - Where is...?

32. La stazione ferroviaria - The railway station

33. L'aeroporto - The airport

34. La fermata dell autobus - The bus halt

35. A sinistra, a destra - Left, right

36. Dritto - Straight ahead

37. Quanto dista...? - How far is...?

38. Quanto tempo ci vuole? - How long does it take?

39. Posso prendere un taxi? - Can I use a taxi?

40. Quanto costa and are a...? - How much does it cost to get to...?

These fundamental Italian phrases will serve as a beneficial basis for conversation throughout your travels or contacts with Italian people. Remember to improve pronunciation and immerse oneself in the language as much as possible to develop your language abilities."

- Cultural Etiquette and Customs

Italy is a nation rich in history, art, and culture, and it's necessary to educate oneself about the local traditions and etiquette while visiting or dealing with Italians. Understanding and following these cultural standards can not only make your visit more pleasurable but also help you develop great ties with the locals. Here are some crucial components of Italian cultural etiquette and traditions to bear in mind:

1. **Greetings and Social Interactions**: - Italians often greet each other with a handshake, particularly when meeting for the first time. Close friends and family members may share kisses on the cheek, commencing with the left cheek.

- It is usual to address persons by their titles and surnames unless they specifically encourage you to use their names. - Italians love personal ties, so take the time to engage in small conversations and show interest in their life. Building connections is typically placed above efficiency.

2. **Dining Etiquette**: - Italians take their food seriously, and dining is a major social occasion. Table etiquette is vital, including using utensils correctly and avoiding resting your elbows on the table. - When invited to someone's house for dinner, it is usual to bring a little present for the host, such as a bottle of wine or flowers. Expressing thanks for the meal is considered polite. - The Italian eating experience is often casual and unhurried, with numerous meals and pauses between each. Rushing through a meal is often frowned upon.

3. **Dress Code**: - Italians prefer to dress nicely and take pleasure in their appearance. When visiting holy locations or upmarket restaurants, it's advised to dress modestly and avoid wearing exposing or beachwear attire. – In more informal situations, such as cafés or outdoor markets, comfortable and fashionable clothes are appropriate.

4. **Personal Space and Gestures**: - Italians are often warm and expressive, employing hand gestures to improve their conversation. However, it's crucial to be careful of personal space and avoid unwanted gestures. - Light physical contact during chats, such as caressing someone's arm, is not prevalent among friends

or close acquaintances. However, it is essential to judge the situation and follow the example of the locals.

5. **Timeliness and Time**: - While Italians admire timeliness in professional and formal contexts, they usually have a more flexible attitude toward time. It is fairly unusual for social gatherings to start a little later than the given hour, so being flexible and patient is crucial.

6. **Cultural Sensitivity**: - Italy has a diversified cultural environment with unique regional identities. It is crucial to be courteous and open-minded about local customs, traditions, and languages, particularly while going outside main tourist destinations.

- Learning a few simple Italian words may go a long way in expressing respect for the local language and culture.

Remember, cultural standards may differ even within Italy, so it's good to notice and adapt to the unique traditions of the place you are in. By displaying respect and understanding, you may develop genuine relationships and have a more fulfilling experience throughout your stay in Italy.

- Safety Tips and Emergency Contacts

Italy is a lovely nation renowned for its rich history, magnificent scenery, and lively culture. Whether you are a resident or a visitor visiting Italy, it's crucial to prioritize your safety and be prepared for any crises that may happen. Here are some detailed safety recommendations and emergency contacts to keep in mind while in Italy:

1. **General Safety Tips**: - Stay cautious of your surroundings, especially in popular tourist locations, since pickpocketing may occur.

- Keep your stuff safe and avoid exhibiting precious goods in public.

- Use recognized transportation providers and be aware of unauthorized taxis.

- Be cautious while crossing roads, since traffic in certain Italian towns may be hectic.

- Follow any municipal restrictions and cautions linked to natural catastrophes or bad weather conditions.

2. **Health and Medical Emergencies**: - In case of a medical emergency, contact the European crisis number 112 for quick help.

- Ensure you have appropriate travel insurance that covers medical expenditures.

- Familiarize oneself with the location of neighboring hospitals or medical institutions.

- Carry important drugs with you, along with a prescription or doctor's note.

- Be mindful of your food and drink consumption to prevent foodborne infections.

3. **Crime and Emergency Services**: - In case of a major crime or emergency, phone the national crisis number 112 to notify the police, ambulance, or fire department.

- Report any incidents or thefts to the local police station and request a copy of the police report for insurance reasons.

- Register with your embassy or consulate upon arrival to obtain information and help if required.

4. **Natural Disasters**: - Italy is prone to earthquakes, especially in the central and southern areas. Familiarize yourself with evacuation protocols and follow any advice from local authorities. - Stay educated about meteorological conditions, particularly during the summer months when forest fires might develop. Follow the advice from local authorities and avoid dangerous regions.

5. **Emergency Contacts**:
- Crisis Assistance: 112

- Authorities: 113
- Medical Emergencies: 112
- Fire Department: 115
- Carabinieri (Military Police): 112 or 112 (English-speaking operators available)

6. **Travel papers and Consular Assistance**: - Keep your passport, visa, and other travel papers safe. Make copies and keep them separately in case of loss or theft.

- Contact your embassy or consulate in Italy for consular help in case of emergency, such as lost or stolen passports.

It's crucial to remember that although this safety advice and emergency contacts might be useful, they should not be considered a complete list. It is always recommended to remain informed of the latest travel warnings, recommendations, and local restrictions from official sources before going to or within Italy.

- Health and Medical Services

Italy is recognized for its rich cultural legacy, stunning scenery, and outstanding food. Alongside these attractions, the nation offers a robust healthcare system that delivers excellent healthcare to both inhabitants and tourists. This guide seeks to present a complete overview of the health and medical services available in Italy, including information on public and private healthcare providers, insurance coverage, emergency services, and healthcare facilities.

1. **Public Healthcare System**: Italy has a universal healthcare system called Servizio Sanitario Nazionale (SSN). It is supported via ordinary taxes and offers healthcare services to all Italian citizens and residents. The SSN is overseen by the Ministry of Health and handled at regional levels.

a. **Primary Care**: The initial point of contact within the public healthcare system is the primary care physician (medico di famiglia). These physicians offer basic medical treatment, preventative services, and referrals to specialists if required.

b. **Specialist Care**: The SSN also covers specialty care, such as consultations with specialists, diagnostic tests, operations, and hospitalizations. However, there may be waiting delays for non-emergency operations.

c. **Prescription drugs**: Prescription drugs are accessible at pharmacies (farmacia) upon presentation of a doctor's prescription. A modest co-payment may apply.

2. **Private Healthcare**: Private healthcare services in Italy are widely accessible and provide speedier access to medical treatment, a greater selection of experts, and more luxurious facilities. Private hospitals and clinics are especially popular among ex-pats and those who desire speedier access to healthcare services.

a. **Private Hospitals**: Private hospitals in Italy offer a comprehensive variety of medical services, including elective procedures, diagnostic testing, and specialty therapies. These institutions frequently have reduced waiting periods and provide more individualized service.

b. **Private Health Insurance**: Private health insurance may augment the public healthcare system in Italy. It gives extra advantages, such as access to private hospitals, choice of physicians, and coverage for treatments not covered by the SSN. It is suggested for expatriates and anyone seeking additional freedom and convenience.

3. **Emergency Medical Services**: In case of medical crises in Italy, urgent medical treatment is provided via emergency number 112. Emergency medical services (EMS) offer prompt response and transfer to the closest hospital. Italy has a well-developed network of hospitals suited to manage emergency patients.

4. **Healthcare Facilities**: Italy is home to several healthcare facilities, including hospitals, clinics, and specialist treatment centers. These facilities vary in size, capacity, and expertise, serving a broad variety of medical requirements.

a. **Hospitals**: Italy has both public and private hospitals, giving complete medical services. Some of the prominent hospitals in Italy include Policlinico Gemelli in Rome, San Raffaele Hospital in Milan, and Careggi Hospital in Florence.

b. **Clinics and Specialized Centers**: Specialized clinics and treatment centers cater to specific medical disciplines, such as cardiology, oncology, orthopedics, and reproductive health. These facilities generally offer state-of-the-art technology and highly specialized medical skills.

5. **Health Insurance**: While public healthcare is provided to all inhabitants in Italy, it is important to acquire health insurance to assure adequate coverage, particularly for non-emergency procedures, private healthcare, and extra services not covered by the SSN. International health insurance plans or private Italian health insurance companies provide many solutions customized to individual requirements.

In conclusion, Italy's healthcare system offers a broad variety of health and medical services to locals and tourists alike. The universal public healthcare system, together with private healthcare choices and a well-developed network of hospitals and clinics, assures access to excellent healthcare. Whether via the public system or private alternatives, residents in Italy may avail themselves of extensive medical services and have peace of mind over their healthcare needs. Residents and tourists need to acquaint themselves with the healthcare system, understand their rights and coverage, and consider purchasing private health insurance for extra advantages. With Italy's commitment to delivering accessible and excellent medical care, citizens can rest assured that their health requirements will be handled in a nation noted for its attention to both cultural heritage and well-being.

- Travel Insurance

Traveling to Italy is a fascinating experience, whether for pleasure, business, or educational interests. To guarantee a comfortable and at-ease journey, it is vital to have enough travel insurance coverage. This thorough guide includes essential information regarding travel insurance for Italy, including its significance, coverage choices, major features, and advice for picking the best policy.

1. **Importance of Travel Insurance**: Travel insurance functions as a safety net, offering financial protection and support in different unexpected scenarios that may arise during your vacation to Italy. It provides coverage for medical emergencies, trip cancellations or interruptions, lost or delayed luggage, and other travel-related problems. Having travel insurance gives you peace of mind and shields you against unexpected charges and inconveniences.

2. **Coverage Options**: Travel insurance packages for Italy generally contain the following coverage options:

a. **Medical Coverage**: This covers expenditures linked to emergency medical care, hospitalizations, prescriptions, and medical evacuations if required. It is vital to verify that the insurance offers appropriate coverage for medical expenditures in Italy, given the country's healthcare costs.

b. **Vacation Cancellation and Interruption**: This coverage reimburses non-refundable charges if your vacation is canceled or cut short due to covered circumstances, such as sickness, accident, or unanticipated occurrences like natural disasters.

c. **Bags and Personal things**: This coverage reimburses you for lost, stolen, or damaged bags and personal things during your trip. It may also pay reimbursement for important things bought in case of delayed luggage arrival.

d. **Travel Delay**: If your trip is severely delayed due to factors beyond your control, travel delay coverage may compensate you for extra hotel, food, and transportation expenditures incurred during the delay.

e. **Emergency help**: Travel insurance generally includes 24/7 emergency help services, offering access to multilingual support, medical referrals, travel counseling, and emergency cash advances.

f. **Personal Liability**: This coverage protects you against possible legal expenditures or damages you may be responsible for, such as unintentional harm to others or property damage.

3. **Major Features to Consider**: When picking a travel insurance package for Italy, consider the following major features:

a. **Medical Coverage Limits**: Ensure that the insurance offers enough coverage for medical expenditures, including emergency medical evacuation and repatriation.

b. **Pre-existing Medical issues**: If you have pre-existing medical issues, determine whether they are covered or need additional coverage and disclosure.

c. **Deductibles and Exclusions**: Understand the deductibles and exclusions mentioned in the insurance. Be mindful of any activities or circumstances not covered, such as extreme sports or high-risk activities.

d. **Journey Duration and Frequency**: Determine if the insurance covers the duration of your journey and if it matches your travel frequency, whether for a single trip or numerous excursions within a given time.

e. **Policy Cost**: Compare premiums, coverage limits, and deductibles to choose a policy that delivers the best value for your requirements.

4. **Guidelines for Selecting the Right Coverage**: Consider the following guidelines when buying travel insurance coverage for Italy:

a. **Assess Your demands**: Evaluate your travel demands, such as the period of your trip, scheduled activities, and personal possessions to establish the coverage requirements.

b. **Compare Multiple Policies**: Obtain quotes from multiple insurance providers and compare coverage, restrictions, and pricing to choose the most suited policy.

c. **Read the Policy Terms and Conditions**: Carefully analyze the policy material, including the terms and conditions, exclusions, and claim processes, to fully understand the coverage and requirements.

d. **Check current Coverage**: Check whether your current health insurance or credit card benefits already include travel-related coverage. This may assist minimize duplicate coverage and unneeded expenditures.

e. **Get Early**: It is recommended to get travel insurance soon after scheduling your trip to take advantage of coverage advantages that may apply before your trip.

In conclusion, travel insurance is a key component in planning a vacation to Italy. It gives financial security, peace of mind, and aid in case of unforeseen occurrences or crises. By studying the coverage choices, major features, and advice for picking the proper insurance, you can secure a safe and worry-free vacation experience in Italy, concentrating on enjoying the country's rich cultural history and magnificent scenery.

CHAPTER 3. Exploring Italy: Top Destinations

- Rome

Rome, frequently referred to as the "Eternal City," is a metropolis rich in history, culture, and architectural wonders. As the capital city of Italy, Rome shows a unique combination of ancient ruins, Renaissance treasures, and lively contemporary life. With a history spanning over 2,500 years, Rome is a city that has seen the rise and fall of empires, the development of civilization, and the blossoming of art, literature, and philosophy. Let's examine the different features that make Rome a unique place.

Historical Significance: Rome was established in 753 BC and went on to become the capital of the powerful Roman Empire. It functioned as the hub of authority, government, and military prowess, shaping the direction of Western culture for centuries. The Roman Forum, a huge archaeological site, shows the remnants of old administrative buildings, temples, and marketplaces, affording a peek into the everyday life of the Roman Empire. The Colosseum, an iconic emblem of Rome, is an amphitheater that historically held gladiatorial combat and magnificent shows.

Religious Heritage: Rome is the spiritual center of Catholicism and the seat of the Pope. The Vatican City, an autonomous city-state inside Rome, is the world's smallest sovereign state and features St. Peter's Basilica, the biggest cathedral in the world. Inside the church sits Michelangelo's beautiful Pietà sculpture, while the Vatican Museums show an astonishing collection of art, including the Sistine Chapel with its famed ceiling murals created by Michelangelo.

Architectural Splendors: The architecture of Rome is a tribute to its rich past. The Pantheon, a well-preserved Roman temple, exhibits the mastery of ancient engineering with its huge dome and oculus. The Trevi Fountain, an opulent Baroque masterpiece, is a renowned tourist attraction where travelers throw a coin to secure their return to Rome. The Spanish Steps, a massive staircase, link the Piazza di Spagna with the Trinità dei Monti church, affording a breathtaking perspective of the city.

Cultural Gems: Rome is a metropolis of art and culture, featuring several outstanding museums and galleries. The Galleria Borghese holds a unique collection of sculptures and paintings, including works by Bernini and Caravaggio. The MAXXI Museum, created by Zaha Hadid, is today's art gallery showcasing unique exhibits. Additionally, the city is home to several piazzas, like Piazza Navona and Piazza del Popolo, where people and visitors come to enjoy the colorful atmosphere, street entertainment, and superb eating experiences.

Culinary Delights: Italian cuisine is recognized worldwide, and Rome is no exception. The city provides a varied variety of gastronomic pleasures, from classic pasta dishes like carbonara and amatriciana to thin-crust Roman-style pizza. Don't miss the chance to sample real gelato, cappuccino, and tiramisu while wandering the twisting alleyways of Rome. Trastevere, a lovely district, is especially recognized for its superb eateries providing Roman cuisine.

Vibrant City Life: Rome easily mixes its historical past with a contemporary and lively environment. The city's streets are dotted with trendy stores, pleasant cafés, and sophisticated pubs. The Campo de' Fiori market is a busy location where residents and tourists may explore kiosks offering fresh vegetables, flowers, and local specialties. The dynamic nighttime scene provides a range of entertainment alternatives, including theaters, clubs, and live music venues.

Surrounding Beauty: Beyond the city boundaries, Rome offers natural and historical grandeur. The Appian Way, one of the most significant historic Roman highways, offers a magnificent environment for a bike ride or walk. The neighboring Castelli Romani area offers a nice getaway from the hectic metropolis. Nestled in the Alban Hills, this region is studded with lovely villages, wineries, and stunning scenery. Visitors may visit the historic town of Frascati, noted for its wine production, and spend a leisurely day in the vineyards, drinking local wines and relishing traditional food.

A short distance from Rome sits the lovely Tivoli, home to two UNESCO World Heritage Sites: Villa d'Este and Hadrian's Villa. Villa d'Este is famed for its exquisite gardens, filled with complex fountains, waterfalls, and lush foliage. Hadrian's Villa, the ancient home of Emperor Hadrian, shows the grandeur of Roman architecture with its huge complex of palaces, temples, and hot baths.

For nature aficionados, the area around Rome provides stunning vistas. The gorgeous Lake Bracciano, situated just northwest of the city, is a wonderful site for boating, swimming, and picnics. The adjacent Regional Park of Bracciano-Martignano gives chances for trekking and discovering pristine natural areas.

Heading south of Rome, the historic harbor city of Ostia Antica awaits. This archaeological site shows the remains of the once-thriving ancient Roman city of Ostia. Visitors may meander around the well-preserved streets, marvel at the mosaics and frescoes, and get insight into everyday life in ancient Rome.

If you have more time to spare, a day excursion to the intriguing remains of Pompeii and the lovely Amalfi Coast is strongly suggested. Although a few hours distant from Rome, these sites provide a look into the old Roman city buried in volcanic ash and the beautiful seaside scenery of Southern Italy.

In conclusion, Rome's surrounding beauty stretches beyond the city itself. Whether you're interested in history, culture, nature, or just seeking a calm vacation, the territory around Rome gives you a plethora of chances to explore and discover. From historic ruins and quaint villages to stunning scenery and gastronomic pleasures, the territory around Rome matches the city's grandeur and provides a truly unique experience.

- Florence

Florence, also known as Firenze in Italian, is a historic and culturally rich city situated in the heart of Tuscany, Italy. Renowned for its spectacular architecture, art treasures, and energetic environment, Florence is regarded as one of the most beautiful towns in the world. From its majestic Renaissance-era structures to its attractive streets and scenic surroundings, Florence gives tourists a riveting combination of history, art, and Italian charm.

History: Florence has a rich and distinguished history that extends back to ancient Roman times. Founded by Julius Caesar in the 1st century BC, the city developed as a hub of trade and commerce. However, it was during the Renaissance era, notably between the 14th and 16th centuries, that Florence attained the height of her cultural and creative accomplishments. The city became a hotbed of intellectual and creative innovation, drawing famous personalities such as Leonardo da Vinci, Michelangelo, and Galileo Galilei.

Art & Culture: Florence is linked with art and is home to some of the world's finest artistic treasures. The city's historic core, a UNESCO World Heritage site, has several museums, churches, and galleries that showcase a remarkable collection of artwork. The Uffizi Gallery, one of the most renowned museums in Florence, displays works by painters including Botticelli, Raphael, and Titian. The Galleria dell'Accademia is another noteworthy museum containing Michelangelo's famous sculpture, David. Florence's Duomo, with its majestic dome constructed by Filippo Brunelleschi, is a remarkable architectural masterpiece that dominates the city's skyline.

Architecture: Florence exhibits a remarkable collection of architectural marvels that reflect its rich past. The Cathedral of Santa Maria del Fiore, popularly known as the Duomo, is a prominent example of Florentine architecture, having a beautiful marble exterior and a captivating interior. The Ponte Vecchio, a medieval stone bridge across the Arno River, is an iconic emblem of the city. It is notable for its stores erected around the bridge, providing jewelry, art, and souvenirs. Palazzo Vecchio, the municipal hall of Florence, shows a remarkable combination of Gothic and Renaissance styles.

Cuisine: Florence is heaven for food lovers, providing a wonderful assortment of Tuscan cuisine. The city's gastronomic treasures include delicious meals like bistecca alla Fiorentina (Florentine steak), ribollita (a robust vegetable soup), and pappa al pomodoro (tomato and bread soup). Visitors may also enjoy a selection of fresh pasta, including the legendary pappardelle al cinghiale (pasta with wild boar sauce). Pair these meals with a drink of Chianti, a renowned Tuscan wine, and you have a truly Florentine gastronomic experience.

Festivals & Events: Florence holds various exciting festivals and events throughout the year, adding to its cultural charm. The most noteworthy event is the Calcio Storico, a historic football match performed in traditional 16th-century clothes. Held annually in June, it blends athletics, spectacle, and historical reenactments. The Explosion of the Cart (Scoppio del Carro) at Easter is another traditional event when a cart laden with pyrotechnics is exploded to guarantee a healthy crop and prosperity for the city.

To neighboring Areas: While Florence itself provides a plethora of sights, the neighboring area of Tuscany is equally worth seeing. Visitors may take day excursions to attractive locations like Siena, noted for its ancient architecture and the famous Palio horse race. The Tuscan region is studded with vineyards and gorgeous scenery, making it perfect for wine excursions and leisurely drives.

Florence is certainly a city that thrills the senses, immersing guests in a world of art, history, and gastronomic pleasures. Its great architecture, rich cultural legacy, and friendly welcome make it an outstanding destination for tourists from throughout the world. Whether you're walking down the Arno River, admiring masterpieces in world-class museums, or relishing traditional Tuscan food, Florence delivers a timeless and captivating experience that grabs the heart and mind.

- Venice

Venice, nicknamed "The Floating City," is a mesmerizing and unique location situated in northeastern Italy. With its picturesque canals, ancient architecture, and rich cultural legacy, Venice has become one of the most recognizable and popular tourist destinations in the world. Let's explore this fascinating city in greater depth.

Geography and Layout:
Venice is set on a network of 118 tiny islands that are divided by canals and linked by bridges. It is situated in the Venetian Lagoon, which spans along the Adriatic Sea. The city itself is constructed on wooden pilings dug deep into the swampy terrain, and it is a magnificent feat of engineering. The major canal, the Grand

Canal, runs through the city and splits it into two parts: the Rialto area and the San Marco district.

History:

Venice has a lengthy and intriguing history that spans back over 1,500 years. It was created in the 5th century AD by refugees escaping assaults on the mainland. Over the years, Venice emerged as a strong maritime republic and a key hub of commerce between Europe and the East. The Venetian Republic developed throughout the Middle Ages and the Renaissance, becoming a rich and prominent city-state.

Architecture:

Venice is recognized for its spectacular architecture, which represents a combination of many styles and influences. The city shows a unique combination of Byzantine, Gothic, and Renaissance architecture characteristics. Its prominent buildings include St. Mark's Basilica, a marvel of Byzantine architecture embellished with beautiful mosaics; the Doge's Palace, a symbol of Venetian power and grandeur; and the Rialto Bridge, an attractive stone footbridge that crosses the Grand Canal.

Canals and Gondolas:

The canals of Venice are its lifeblood and a distinctive element of the city. These streams, which act as roadways, offer an appealing mode of transit. Gondolas, classic Venetian rowing boats, have become a symbol of Venice. They were previously utilized by the city's wealthy, but now they provide a romantic and leisurely way to tour the canals and absorb the city's ambiance.

Venetian Culture:

Venice has a dynamic and unique culture that has been formed by its history and geography. The city has been a center of creative and intellectual creation, giving birth to great luminaries such as Titian, Tintoretto, and Vivaldi. The Venetian Carnival, conducted yearly, is a celebration of masks, costumes, and extravagant activities that trace back to the city's ancient origins. Venice is also famed for its glassmaking on the island of Murano, where artists manufacture beautiful glassware using ancient processes.

Venetian Cuisine:

Venetian cuisine is inspired by its marine setting and the rich agricultural legacy of the neighboring Veneto area. Seafood plays a key part in Venetian meals, with delicacies like sarde in saor (marinated sardines), baccalà mantecato (creamed salted cod), and risotto al nero di sepia (squid ink rice). Other local delights include Cicchetti, tiny plates of savory nibbles comparable to Spanish tapas, and tiramisu, a favorite Italian dessert.

Tourism and Conservation:

Venice is a prominent tourist attraction, receiving millions of people each year. While tourism has provided economic advantages, it has also caused issues for the city. The enormous number of tourists might strain the sensitive ecology and put pressure on the city's infrastructure. Additionally, the increasing sea levels and erosion threaten the long-term survival of Venice. Efforts are being done to conserve the city's cultural legacy and overcome these difficulties, including the MOSE project, which tries to defend the city from the high seas.

Conclusion:

Venice is a city unlike any other, with its network of canals, breathtaking architecture, and rich history. It continues to draw tourists from throughout the globe with its particular appeal and allure. Whether you explore its small streets and scenic squares, take a gondola ride along the canals, or immerse yourself in its cultural riches, Venice guarantees an extraordinary experience that will leave you with lasting memories.

- Milan

Milan, the fashion capital of Italy and a worldwide hub of culture and trade, is a city with a rich past and a dynamic modern attitude. Located in the Lombardy area of northern Italy, Milan is recognized for its spectacular architecture, outstanding museums, elite shopping, and busy commercial center. Let's go into the entire material about Milan, covering its history, culture, sights, gastronomy, and more.

1. **History**: Milan has a history that stretches over two millennia. Founded by the Celts in the 4th century BC, it became a wealthy Roman metropolis known as Mediolanum. During the Middle Ages, Milan was a strong city-state governed by the Visconti and Sforza dynasties. It functioned as a key hub for Renaissance art and culture, drawing great painters like Leonardo da Vinci. In the ensuing decades, Milan passed through periods of foreign dominance and witnessed substantial industrial

and economic progress, notably during the post-World War II era.

2. **Architecture**: Milan's architecture is a stunning combination of old and contemporary forms. The city features a multitude of spectacular structures, including the famed Gothic church, the Duomo di Milano. This majestic cathedral is one of the biggest in the world and contains ornate spires, sculptures, and gorgeous stained glass windows. Another architectural jewel is the famous Galleria Vittorio Emanuele II, a magnificent 19th-century retail arcade famed for its extravagant iron and glass ceiling. Other prominent monuments are the Sforza Castle, Teatro alla Scala (one of the world's premier opera theaters), and the new skyscrapers of the Porta Nuova neighborhood.

3. **Culture & Arts**: Milan is a cultural center, providing a profusion of museums, galleries, and theaters. The city is home to several world-class art collections, including the classic picture "The Last Supper" by Leonardo da Vinci, located in the Convent of Santa Maria delle Grazie. The Pinacoteca di Brera displays a large collection of Italian Renaissance art, while the Museo del Novecento shows 20th-century

masterpieces. Milan also organizes several fashion and design events, such as Milan Fashion Week and the Salone del Mobile, strengthening its status as a trailblazer in the fashion and design sectors.

4. **Shopping**: Milan is renowned for high-end fashion and luxury shopping. The city's Quadrilatero della Moda (Fashion Quadrilateral) is an affluent shopping zone, with designer stores from known labels like Prada, Gucci, Armani, and Versace. Via Monte Napoleone is notably noted for its premium fashion businesses. Additionally, Milan provides more accessible retail opportunities, including major shopping districts like Corso Buenos Aires and Corso Vittorio Emanuele II. The city also features outlet malls, such as Serravalle Designer Outlet, where tourists may discover designer items at cheap costs.

5. **Food**: Milanese food reflects the city's rich gastronomic past. Traditional Milanese foods include risotto alla Milanese (saffron-infused risotto), ossobuco (braised veal shanks), and cotoletta alla Milanese (breaded and fried veal cutlet). Don't miss out on sampling panettone, a delicious bread loaf commonly consumed during the Christmas season. Milan is also

recognized for its strong café culture, with iconic cafés like Caffè Cova and Caffè Sambuco acting as meeting places for residents and tourists alike.

6. **Green places**: Despite being a hectic town, Milan has various green places where tourists may rest and decompress. Parco Sempione, situated behind the Sforza Castle, is a beautiful park with rich gardens, a lake, and breathtaking vistas. Giardini Pubblici Indro Montanelli is another magnificent park, with a medieval mansion, a planetarium, and a natural history museum. Moreover, the Bosco Verticale (Vertical Forest) is an innovative architectural project consisting of two residential buildings covered with over 900 trees, giving a distinctive and eco-friendly urban environment.

7. **Events and Festivals**: Milan holds many events and festivals throughout the year. Milan Fashion Week, held twice a year, invites worldwide designers, celebrities, and fashion fans to experience the newest trends and collections. The Salone del Mobile is a famous furniture and interior design expo that gathers experts and design aficionados from across the world. Other prominent events include the

Milan Film Festival, the JazzMi music festival, and the La Scala Opera Season.

8. **Day Trips**: Milan provides a good base for visiting local sights. Just a short train trip away, you may explore the gorgeous town of Como, noted for its magnificent lake and charming medieval center. Bergamo, with its ancient old center and panoramic views from the Città Alta, is another popular day travel choice. Verona, famed for its Roman amphitheater and associated with Shakespeare's "Romeo and Juliet," is also within reach. These sites provide a nice change of scenery from the hectic metropolis.

In conclusion, Milan is a mesmerizing city that perfectly integrates its rich historical legacy with a contemporary and active lifestyle. From its breathtaking architecture and world-class museums to its famous fashion scene and scrumptious food, Milan has plenty to offer every tourist. Whether you're a cultural buff, a fashion lover, or a gourmet, Milan will leave you with memorable memories and a profound appreciation for its distinct charm.

- **Naples**

Naples, often known as Napoli in Italian, is a bustling and ancient city situated in southern Italy. It is the capital of the Campania region and the third-biggest municipality in Italy, after Rome and Milan. Naples is famed for its rich history, gorgeous architecture, cultural legacy, wonderful food, and spectacular views of the Bay of Naples and Mount Vesuvius. Let's go into the entire material about Naples, examining its history, culture, attractions, food, and more.

1. **History and Culture**:

Naples has a history that extends back more than 2,800 years. It was created by the ancient Greeks in the 8th century BC and has since been affected by different civilizations, including the Romans, Byzantines, Normans, Swabians, Aragonese, and Bourbons. This rich historical backdrop has left an everlasting effect on the city's architecture, art, and culture.

The old city of Naples, a UNESCO World Heritage site, is a treasure trove of architectural masterpieces. Piazza del Plebiscito, the city's principal plaza, contains the Royal Palace and the beautiful San Francesco di Paola cathedral. Castel Nuovo, a medieval castle, and Castel dell'Ovo, an old fortification, defend the city's shoreline.

Naples is also recognized for its museums and art galleries, such as the National Archaeological Museum, which has an enormous collection of ancient Roman antiquities, including the famed Farnese Bull. The Museo di Capodimonte shows Renaissance and Baroque art, while the Naples Underground gives a unique insight into the city's underground tunnels and cisterns.

2. **Landmarks and Attractions**:

In addition to its historical monuments, Naples features several sights and attractions that enchant tourists. One of the most memorable sites is Mount Vesuvius, the active volcano that famously devastated the ancient city of Pompeii in 79 AD. It is possible to trek to the crater and enjoy panoramic views of the surrounding region.

The remains of Pompeii, situated near Naples, give an unparalleled view of ancient Roman life. Walking around the marvelously maintained streets, residences, and public buildings of this historic city is a mesmerizing experience.

Another must-visit attraction is the Royal Royal of Caserta, a gigantic royal complex with gorgeous gardens. Built in the 18th century for the Bourbon rulers, it is commonly referred to as the "Versailles of Italy."

For those seeking natural beauty, the Amalfi Coast, situated just south of Naples, is a dream getaway. The charming villages of Positano, Amalfi, and Ravello, set on towering cliffs overlooking the turquoise Mediterranean Sea, provide spectacular vistas and wonderful experiences.

3. **Cuisine**:

Naples is generally credited as the home of pizza, and its food is known worldwide. Neapolitan pizza, with its thin, soft dough and simple but delectable toppings, has become a hallmark of Italian food. Visitors may sample real pizza Margherita or Napoli-style calzones at the city's myriad pizzerias.

Apart from pizza, Naples provides a vast assortment of gastronomic delicacies. Pasta dishes like spaghetti alle vongole (spaghetti with clams) and gnocchi alla sorrentina (potato dumplings with tomato sauce and cheese) are popular alternatives. Seafood aficionados may luxuriate in fresh catches from the neighboring

Gulf of Naples, including octopus, mussels, and anchovies.

Naples is also famed for its street cuisine. Try the delectable sfogliatelle (pastry stuffed with sweet ricotta) or the deep-fried pizza known as pizza fritta. And don't forget to try the local espresso or luxuriate with creamy gelato for a fantastic finale to a gourmet trip.

4. Festivals and Traditions:

Naples is a city of strong customs and exuberant events. One of the most notable events is the yearly celebration of San Gennaro, the patron saint of Naples. Held on September 19th, citizens congregate at the Naples Cathedral to watch the "miracle of San Gennaro," when the dried blood of the saint liquefies, indicating good fortune for the city.

During Christmas, Naples comes alive with colorful nativity scenes known as gifts. The artists of Naples are known for their meticulous handiwork, and these beautiful nativity scenes can be seen throughout the city.

5. Surrounding Areas:

Naples provides a gateway to numerous great attractions in the area. Along with Pompeii and the Amalfi Coast, the adjacent island of Capri is a popular day trip destination. With its magnificent surroundings, crystal-clear seas, and the famed Blue Grotto, Capri provides an exquisite refuge from the hectic metropolis.

For history aficionados, a visit to the ancient sites of Herculaneum and Paestum is strongly advised. Herculaneum, like Pompeii, was devastated by the eruption of Mount Vesuvius and boasts well-preserved remains. Paestum, on the other hand, features outstanding Greek temples going back to the 6th century BC.

In conclusion, Naples is a compelling city that enthralls tourists with its rich history, lively culture, and exquisite food. Whether you're visiting its historic ruins, delighting in its culinary pleasures, or just wandering through its busy streets, Naples provides a unique and wonderful experience that will leave you with lasting memories.

- Sicily

Sicily is a mesmerizing and diversified island situated in the southern region of Italy, in the Mediterranean Sea. With its rich history, gorgeous scenery, wonderful food, and kind hospitality, Sicily has long been a favorite destination for tourists seeking a unique and unforgettable experience. Let's explore the complete substance of this interesting island.

Geography and Location:

Sicily is the biggest island in the Mediterranean, encompassing an area of roughly 25,711 square kilometers (9,927 square miles). It is separated from the Italian mainland by the Strait of Messina, which is barely 3 kilometers (1.9 miles) wide at its narrowest point. The island is ideally placed at the crossroads of Europe and Africa, making it a melting pot of cultures and influences.

History and Cultural Significance:

Sicily has a rich and complicated history that spans over 3,000 years. It was formerly populated by indigenous peoples, including the Sicani, Sicels, and Elymians. The island eventually became a Greek colony and thrived under the administration of numerous Greek city-states, most notably Syracuse. During the Punic Wars, Sicily fell under Roman authority and became an important agricultural and cultural center of the Roman Empire.

Over the ages, Sicily was dominated by various powers, including the Vandals, Ostrogoths, Byzantines, Arabs, Normans, Swabians,

Angevins, Aragonese, and Bourbons. Each of these civilizations left its stamp on the island, adding to its unique cultural legacy.

Architecture and Landmarks:

Sicily features an astounding assortment of architectural beauties that highlight its historical and cultural relevance. The Valley of the Temples, situated near Agrigento, is a UNESCO World Heritage site that features some of the best-preserved Greek temples outside of Greece. The Cathedral of Monreale, with its beautiful Byzantine mosaics, is another must-visit destination.

Other significant sites are the ancient theater of Taormina, the Norman Palace and Palatine Chapel in Palermo, the Baroque settlements of Noto and Ragusa, and the well-preserved Greek remains of Selinunte and Segesta.

Natural Beauty and Landscapes:

Sicily is recognized for its stunning scenery, ranging from lovely coasts to jagged mountains. The island is dominated by Mount Etna, one of the world's most active volcanoes. Its towering presence provides awe-inspiring vistas and fantastic trekking options.

Sicily's coastline runs for more than 1,000 kilometers (620 miles) and includes gorgeous beaches, crystal-clear waters, and lovely coastal villages. The Aeolian Islands, a UNESCO World Heritage site, is a volcanic archipelago off the northern coast of Sicily, recognized for its magnificent beauty and distinctive geological characteristics.

Inland, you'll discover lush vineyards, olive gardens, citrus orchards, and lovely hilltop towns hidden between rolling hills. The landscapes of Sicily give numerous options for outdoor activities, such as hiking, cycling, and visiting natural reserves.

Cuisine:

Sicilian food is a delicious combination of tastes inspired by its rich past. The island's lush soil and Mediterranean climate create a profusion of fresh foods, culminating in a rich culinary culture. Sicilian cuisine is recognized for its plentiful use of fish, sun-ripened tomatoes, eggplants, citrus fruits, and fragrant herbs.

Must-try foods include arancini (fried rice balls), pasta alla Norma (pasta with eggplant, tomatoes, and ricotta salata), caponata (a sweet and sour eggplant relish), cannoli (crispy pastry tubes filled with sweet ricotta), and granita (a pleasant semi-frozen dessert).

Festivals and Traditions:
Sicily is recognized for its colorful festivals and customs, which represent the island's strong feeling of community and cultural history. The Feast of Saint Agatha in Catania is one of the major religious celebrations in Sicily, gathering thousands of devotees who pay respect to the city's patron saint.

Carnival festivities, notably in the municipality of Acireale, are noted for their ornate floats, colorful costumes, and energetic processions. Other important festivals are the Infiorata flower festival in Noto, the Cous Cous Fest in San Vito Lo Capo, and the Almond Blossom Festival in Agrigento.

Conclusion:
Sicily is a mesmerizing island that provides a perfect combination of history, culture, natural beauty, and gastronomic pleasures. From its ancient Greek temples to its charming seaside villages, there is something to fascinate every tourist. Whether you're visiting its historical sites, delighting in its excellent food, or just basking in the sun on its magnificent beaches, Sicily guarantees an amazing experience that will leave you wishing to return.

- Cinque Terre

Cinque Terre, or "Five Lands" in Italian, is a scenic location situated along the rough coastline of the Italian Riviera in the Liguria region. It features five beautiful fishing villages: Monterosso al Mare, Vernazza, Corniglia, Manarola, and Riomaggiore. These settlements are famed for their spectacular natural beauty, preserved architecture, and distinctive character, making Cinque Terre one of the most charming locations in Italy.

1. **Monterosso al Mare**: Monterosso al Mare is the biggest and most visited hamlet in Cinque Terre. It is recognized for its magnificent beaches, crystal-clear seas, and dynamic environment. The hamlet is separated into two parts: the old town with its narrow streets and ancient buildings, and the new town with its contemporary conveniences and beachside resorts.

2. **Vernazza**: Vernazza is a lovely hamlet noted by its colorful buildings constructed on cliffs. It boasts a modest natural harbor that was formerly a lively commercial port. The hamlet boasts spectacular vistas, a gorgeous main

plaza, and a historic castle that overlooks the town.

3. **Corniglia**: Perched on a peninsula, Corniglia is the only settlement in Cinque Terre that is not immediately accessible from the sea. It is located on top of a hill, surrounded by terraced vineyards and beautiful flora. Corniglia is recognized for its calm, panoramic vistas, and quaint small lanes.

4. **Manarola**: Manarola is famed for its postcard-perfect landscape and is frequently called the most charming town in Cinque Terre. It has colorful houses clinging to the cliffs, a lovely port, and a busy waterfront with attractive restaurants and cafés.

5. **Riomaggiore**: Riomaggiore is the southernmost settlement in Cinque Terre and provides a lovely combination of historic charm and natural beauty. Its colorful houses tumble down the slope to the lovely bay, providing a charming and appealing backdrop. Riomaggiore also gives access to the famed Via dell'Amore (Lover's Lane), a gorgeous seaside walk linking it to Manarola.

Apart from the distinctive appeal of each hamlet, the whole Cinque Terre area is a UNESCO World Heritage Site and a national park. The craggy cliffs, terraced vineyards, and gorgeous routes that link the settlements make it a heaven for nature lovers and hikers. The paths, especially the famed Sentiero Azzurro (Blue Path), provide beautiful views of the coastline, verdant landscapes, and the Mediterranean Sea.

The gastronomy of Cinque Terre is another highlight. Being a seaside location, seafood plays a key part in the local meals. Anchovies, squid, and other fresh catches are regularly used in traditional Ligurian cuisine. The area is also famed for its pesto sauce, which is created from locally produced basil, pine nuts, olive oil, and Parmesan cheese.

When visiting Cinque Terre, it is crucial to respect the delicate nature and the local inhabitants. Cars are not permitted in the villages, and it is encouraged to explore the region on foot or by rail. The Cinque Terre Card is a simple card that offers access to the railways, hiking trails, and admittance to the park.

In conclusion, Cinque Terre is a mesmerizing location that provides a unique combination of natural beauty, cultural legacy, and gourmet pleasures. Its five lovely settlements, surrounded by rocky cliffs and blue seas, make a memorable experience for tourists. Whether you're a nature enthusiast, a history buff, or a culinary lover, Cinque Terre is guaranteed to leave you with lasting memories of its beautiful splendor.

- Amalfi Coast

The Amalfi Coast is a gorgeous and attractive location situated in the southern section of Italy, along the shoreline of the Salerno Gulf in the Campania province. Famous for its spectacular beauty, picturesque cliffside villages, and transparent blue seas, the Amalfi Coast has become one of the most desired destinations for tourists from across the globe.

Stretching for nearly 50 kilometers (31 miles), the Amalfi Coast is a UNESCO World Heritage Site famed for its spectacular scenery, cliffs, and colorful terraced settlements that appear to defy gravity. The coast is named for the town of Amalfi, which was once a great maritime republic during the Middle Ages and played a vital role in trade and commerce in the Mediterranean.

One of the great attractions of the Amalfi Coast is its magnificent panoramic drives. The coastal road, known as the Amalfi Drive or the SS163, makes its way down the cliffside, affording magnificent views of the Mediterranean Sea below. The route is noted for its hairpin twists, tiny tunnels, and spectacular panoramas of the craggy coastline and beautiful settlements.

The Amalfi Coast is home to various wonderful towns and villages, each with its distinct character and charm. Positano, with its pastel-colored buildings tumbling down the cliffside, is undoubtedly the most famous and attractive hamlet on the coast. Its small streets, boutique stores, and breathtaking beach make it a must-visit location.

Amalfi, the eponymous town of the coast, is a historic jewel with a rich past. Here, you may tour the beautiful Cathedral of St. Andrew, a remarkable 9th-century edifice that dominates the main plaza. The town also provides stunning beaches, picturesque streets, and a bustling environment.

Ravello, positioned high above the sea, is famed for its beautiful vistas and its gorgeous mansions and gardens. Villa Rufolo and Villa Cimbrone are two noteworthy sights in Ravello, providing tourists with spectacular landscapes and gorgeous gardens that have inspired painters and poets for ages.

Another wonderful hamlet worth seeing is Praiano, a calmer and less crowded alternative to some of the more famous cities. Its beautiful environment, picturesque beach coves, and spectacular sunsets make it a hidden treasure on the coast.

In addition to its lovely villages, the Amalfi Coast features countless pristine beaches and secluded coves. The crystal-clear waters entice people to swim, snorkel, and sunbathe. Some of the prominent beaches are Spiaggia Grande in Positano and Marina Grande in Amalfi.

Apart from its natural splendor, the Amalfi Coast provides a rich cultural and gastronomic experience. The area is famed for its exquisite gastronomy, which highlights fresh seafood, sun-ripened fruits and vegetables, local cheeses, and limoncello, a lemon liqueur created from the region's famous lemons. Indulge in classic delicacies like spaghetti alle vongole (spaghetti with clams), parmigiana di melanzane (eggplant Parmesan), and tagliatelle (a local pastry).

The Amalfi Coast is not solely a summer attraction. It has a moderate environment throughout the year, making it a desirable spot to visit even during the spring and fall seasons when the weather is lovely, and the crowds are lower. Hiking enthusiasts may explore the famed "Path of the Gods" (Sentiero degli Dei), a picturesque route that gives stunning views of the shoreline and the surrounding mountains.

To properly enjoy the splendor of the Amalfi Coast, try taking a boat trip around the coastline or hiring a private boat to explore secret caves and isolated beaches. Capri, the lovely island lying just off the shore, is a popular day trip location from the Amalfi Coast and offers breathtaking vistas, elegant shops, and the famed Blue Grotto.

In conclusion, the Amalfi Coast is a genuine jewel of Italy, presenting a wonderful combination of natural beauty, cultural legacy, and gastronomic pleasures. Whether you are seeking leisure on the beaches, exploration of lovely villages, or just immersing yourself in the stunning surroundings, the Amalfi Coast guarantees a memorable experience that will leave you enchanted by its timeless beauty.

-Tuscany

Tuscany, situated in central Italy, is a region famed for its breathtaking landscapes, rich history, cultural legacy, artistic masterpieces, and world-class food. From rolling hills and vineyards to attractive towns and ancient cities, Tuscany provides a broad selection of experiences for travelers. Let's plunge into the complete material of Tuscany.

1. **Geographical and Historical Background**: Tuscany, known as "Toscana" in Italian, is located in central Italy, bordering the Tyrrhenian Sea to the west. It includes an area of around 23,000 square kilometers and is split into 10 provinces, including Florence, Siena, Pisa, Lucca, and Arezzo. The area is defined by its diverse geography, comprising the Apennine Mountains in the east, coastal plains in the west, and undulating hills in the center.

Tuscany has a rich history extending back to ancient times when it was inhabited by the Etruscans, a pre-Roman culture. The area developed throughout the Renaissance, with towns like Florence becoming prominent centers of art, culture, and trade. Tuscany has been home to notable personalities such as

Leonardo da Vinci, Michelangelo, Galileo Galilei, and Dante Alighieri, who impacted the region's cultural and intellectual heritage.

2. **Cities and Towns**: Tuscany is sprinkled with various attractive cities and towns, each having its distinct features and ambiance. Here are some of the more prominent ones:

- **Florence**: The capital city of Tuscany and the cradle of the Renaissance, Florence is a treasure trove of art and architecture. The renowned Duomo, Uffizi Gallery, Ponte Vecchio, and David by Michelangelo in the Academy Museum are must-see sites.

- **Siena**: Known for its ancient architecture and the famed Palio horse race, Siena is a UNESCO World Heritage site. The majestic Piazza del Campo, the Duomo, and the small alleyways of the medieval center are highlights.

- **Pisa**: Home to the famed Leaning Tower, Pisa draws people from throughout the globe. Besides the Leaning Tower, the Piazza dei Miracoli complex comprises the Duomo, Baptistery, and Camposanto Monumentale.

- **Lucca**: Encircled by well-preserved Renaissance-era walls, Lucca provides a pleasant and easygoing environment. The city is noted for its preserved ancient core, tree-lined walls for bike or strolling, and the spectacular Lucca Cathedral.

- **San Gimignano**: Famous for its ancient towers, San Gimignano is a lovely hilltop village. Its well-preserved medieval buildings and breathtaking views of the surrounding countryside make it a must-visit location.

- **Cortona**: Perched on a hill above the Val di Chiana, Cortona is a picturesque town noted for its Etruscan remnants, medieval fortifications, and panoramic panoramas. It achieved worldwide popularity with the novel and movie "Under the Tuscan Sun."

3. **Natural Landscapes**: Tuscany's natural beauty is a big magnet for travelers. The area is characterized by undulating hills, vineyards, cypress-lined roads, and sunflower fields. The Val d'Orcia, a UNESCO World Heritage site, is recognized for its stunning vistas, while the Chianti wine area provides attractive drives across vineyard-dotted hills. The Maremma, with its unspoiled coastline, pine woods, and natural reserves, is great for environment enthusiasts.

4. **Art and Culture**: Tuscany has played a crucial role in the development of art and

culture throughout the ages. Florence, in particular, is a treasure trove of creative marvels. The Uffizi Gallery features pieces by Botticelli, Leonardo da Vinci, Michelangelo, and Raphael, among others. The Galleria dell'Accademia is home to Michelangelo's iconic sculpture of David. Other art locations include the Pitti Palace, Bargello Museum, and the Boboli Gardens.

Apart from art, Tuscany conducts several cultural events and festivals throughout the year. The Palio di Siena, an exciting horse race hosted in the Piazza del Campo, is a pinnacle of Sienese history. The Lucca Summer Festival gathers globally known performers, while the Puccini Festival in Torre del Lago honors the works of the legendary composer Giacomo Puccini.

5. **Gastronomy & Wine**: Tuscany is associated with superb food and world-renowned wines. The area has a strong culinary legacy with delicacies like Florentine steak (bistecca alla Fiorentina), ribollita (a hearty vegetable soup), pappa al pomodoro (tomato and bread soup), and pici pasta.

Tuscan wine, notably Chianti, has earned a worldwide reputation. The vineyards in the

Chianti Classico area provide wine tastings and excursions. Other noteworthy wine districts include Montalcino, noted for its Brunello wine, and Montepulciano, famous for Vino Nobile.

6. **Outdoor Activities and Recreation**: Tuscany provides abundant chances for outdoor lovers. The area is crisscrossed with hiking and bicycle routes, affording spectacular views of the landscape. The Apuan Alps give hiking and climbing possibilities, while the shore provides water activities including sailing, windsurfing, and diving. The thermal baths at Saturnia, Bagno Vignoni, and Montecatini Terme are famous for relaxation and well-being.

7. **Practical Information**: - Tuscany is well-connected by air, having international airports in Florence, Pisa, and Grosseto.

- The ideal method to tour Tuscany is by automobile since it gives the flexibility to visit smaller towns and rural regions.

- The area has a Mediterranean climate, with hot summers and moderate winters. Spring and fall are often nice and less congested.

- Italian is the official language, however, English is frequently used in tourist areas.

- Tuscany provides a choice of lodging alternatives, from luxury hotels to agriturismos (farm stays) and lovely guesthouses.

In conclusion, Tuscany's attractiveness rests in its beautiful combination of spectacular vistas, cultural riches, rich history, wonderful food, and friendly hospitality. Whether you're visiting its ancient towns, relishing its culinary pleasures, or just immersing yourself in its natural beauty, Tuscany provides an exceptional experience for every tourist.

- The Italian Lakes

The Italian Lakes region is a stunningly gorgeous location situated in the northern section of Italy. Nestled in the foothills of the Alps, this area is recognized for its spectacular natural scenery, attractive towns, and calm lakes. The Italian Lakes provide a great blend of natural beauty, rich history, and cultural attractions, making it a favorite destination for people from across the globe.

There are five important lakes in the area, each with its distinctive appeal and character: Lake Como, Lake Maggiore, Lake Garda, Lake Orta, and Lake Iseo. Let's investigate these lakes in greater detail:

1. **Lake Como**: Situated in Lombardy, Lake Como is the most renowned and luxurious of the Italian Lakes. Surrounded by stunning mountains, the lake is noted for its crystal-clear blue waters and elegant mansions. The picturesque villages of Bellagio, Varenna, and Como offer tiny streets, exquisite architecture, and spectacular vistas. Visitors may take boat cruises across the lake, climb the neighboring hills, or just rest and enjoy the tranquil surroundings.

2. **Lake Maggiore**: Straddling the border between Italy and Switzerland, Lake Maggiore is the second-largest lake in Italy. It features a moderate temperature, rich greenery, and a variety of beautiful gardens, including the famed Borromean Islands. Isola Bella, with its spectacular Baroque castle and terraced gardens, is a must-visit site. Stresa, the major town on the lake, provides a wonderful promenade and spectacular views of the surrounding mountains.

3. **Lake Garda**: The biggest lake in Italy, Lake Garda is situated in the districts of Lombardy, Veneto, and Trentino. Its diversified scenery

includes stunning beaches, cliffs, and picturesque lakeside villages. Sirmione, with its ancient castle and hot springs, is a popular vacation. Garda, Bardolino, and Malcesine are additional gorgeous towns worth investigating. Outdoor enthusiasts may enjoy windsurfing, sailing, hiking, and mountain biking in this region.

4. **Lake Orta**: Often ignored by visitors, Lake Orta is a hidden treasure situated west of Lake Maggiore. It provides a quiet and romantic ambiance, with the picturesque island of San Giulio in its heart. Orta San Giulio, the major town, is famed for its small cobblestone alleys, colorful houses, and breathtaking views of the lake. A visit to the Sacro Monte di Orta, a UNESCO World Heritage site with a chain of chapels, is strongly recommended.

5. **Lake Iseo**: Located between Lake Como and Lake Garda, Lake Iseo is the smallest of the Italian Lakes. It is recognized for its tranquil surroundings and pristine beauty. Monte Isola, a steep island in the lake, is a popular site for trekking and riding. The village of Iseo boasts a picturesque seaside promenade and superb local cuisine, notably its famed seafood specialties.

Apart from the lakes themselves, the area provides various additional attractions. Wine enthusiasts may tour the vineyards and wineries of Franciacorta, noted for its sparkling wines. The cities of Milan and Bergamo are within easy reach and provide a plethora of cultural and historical landmarks, shopping possibilities, and exciting nightlife.

In conclusion, the Italian Lakes area is a veritable paradise for nature lovers, history fans, and those seeking leisure. With its magnificent lakes, quaint villages, and a vast choice of activities, it delivers a great combination of natural beauty and cultural depth. Whether you're hoping to visit historical monuments, participate in water sports, or just rest among stunning landscapes, the Italian Lakes won't disappoint.

CHAPTER 4. Must-See Attractions and Landmarks

- Colosseum, Rome

The Colosseum, also known as the Flavian Amphitheatre, is a renowned historic structure situated in the city of Rome, Italy. It is regarded as one of the finest architectural and technical accomplishments of the Roman Empire and stands as a symbol of Rome's rich history and magnificence. Here is a thorough account of the Colosseum, covering its history, architecture, importance, and cultural effect.

1. History: The building of the Colosseum started in 72 AD during the administration of Vespasian, the Emperor of Rome, and was finally completed in eighty AD under the rule of his son, Emperor Titus. It was erected on the site of Nero's magnificent palace complex, the Domus Aurea, which was largely demolished following his death. The Colosseum was constructed as a gift to the people of Rome, serving as a venue for different spectacles and public events.

2. Architecture: The Colosseum is an elliptical amphitheater with a diameter of 573 meters (1,880 feet), a length of 187 meters (610 feet), and a width of 156 meters (512 feet). It stands roughly 48 meters (157 feet) tall, once having four stories. The outside walls are composed of travertine stone, while the inside has brick and concrete construction.

The amphitheater could hold an estimated 50,000 to 80,000 people, who would congregate to see gladiatorial competitions, fake naval battles, animal hunts, and other types of entertainment. The seating arrangement represented the Roman social order, with the finest seats designated for the aristocracy and the upper classes, while the less fortunate individuals inhabited the top levels.

3. Significance: The Colosseum was a symbol of the Roman Empire's strength, riches, and architectural talent. It highlighted the grandeur and richness of Rome and showed the empire's capacity to create expensive shows for its inhabitants. The amphitheater served a key function in establishing social solidarity, diverting the public from political and social difficulties, and consolidating the emperor's power.

4. Cultural Impact: The Colosseum contains great cultural importance and has left an everlasting effect on human history. It has become a symbol not just of ancient Rome but also of the survival and heritage of the Roman civilization. Its architecture has influenced other buildings and structures over the years, making it a timeless emblem of architectural perfection.

Today, the Colosseum remains one of the most prominent tourist sites in Rome, bringing millions of tourists from across the globe. It is classified as a UNESCO World Heritage site and serves as a striking reminder of the ancient world's magnificence and the need of protecting cultural heritage.

5. Restoration and Preservation: Over the decades, the Colosseum suffered from neglect, aging, and damage caused by earthquakes and theft. However, considerable repair work has been conducted to protect this historic site. In recent years, there have been measures to clean the façade, stabilize the building, and enhance tourist amenities, guaranteeing that future generations may continue to experience the Colosseum's majesty.

In conclusion, the Colosseum endures as a tribute to the grandeur and architectural genius of ancient Rome. Its historical importance, cultural effect, and ongoing legacy make it an essential stop site for everyone interested in Roman history and architecture. The Colosseum continues to attract tourists with its amazing presence, offering a physical connection to the astonishing accomplishments of one of the world's greatest civilizations.

- Vatican City

Vatican City, officially referred to as the Vatican Metropolitan State is an autonomous city-state enclaved inside Rome, Italy. It is the smallest internationally recognized sovereign state in the world by both land and population. Vatican City enjoys a unique position as the spiritual and administrative headquarters of the Roman Catholic Church and is the home of the Pope, the leader of the global Catholic Church. With its rich history, cultural relevance, and religious prominence, Vatican City draws millions of people from across the world each year. Here is extensive material about Vatican City, including its history, government, attractions, and more.

History:

The history of Vatican City extends back to ancient times when the territory was part of the Roman Empire. In the 4th century, Emperor Constantine authorized Christianity, and the first Christian basilicas were erected in the neighborhood. However, the roots of the Vatican as a separate institution may be traced to the Lateran Treaty of 1929, which addressed the "Roman Question" between the Holy See and the Kingdom of Italy.

Establishment of Vatican City State:

Under the Lateran Treaty, Vatican City was formed as an autonomous city-state inside Rome. This treaty acknowledged the complete sovereignty of the Holy See over Vatican City, providing it the ability to exercise control over its territory and internal affairs. The Pope, as the head of the Roman Catholic Church, acts as the ruler of Vatican City.

Geography and Size:

Vatican City comprises an area of around 44 hectares (110 acres) inside the city of Rome,

Italy. It is situated on Vatican Hill, northwest of the Tiber River, and is surrounded by Rome. Despite its modest size, Vatican City is home to some spectacular monuments and notable religious and cultural organizations.

Governance:

The administration of Vatican City is an absolute monarchy, with the Pope as the head of state. The Pope enjoys complete legislative, executive, and judicial powers inside the city-state. The Pope is chosen by the College of Cardinals, who convene in the Sistine Chapel during a papal conclave. The Secretary of State acts as the primary government official, aiding the Pope in the administration of Vatican City.

Religious Significance:

Vatican City is the spiritual center of the Roman Catholic Church and bears tremendous religious importance for Catholics worldwide. The Vatican is the seat of the Pope, who is regarded as the successor of Saint Peter, the first Bishop of Rome. It is also the home of Saint Peter's Basilica, one of the most significant

Catholic pilgrimage destinations and the biggest cathedral in the world.

Attractions in Vatican City:

Vatican City provides several attractions that entice tourists from varied origins and interests. Some of the significant highlights include:

1. **St. Peter's Basilica:** This landmark church is a marvel of Renaissance design and the burial location of Saint Peter. Its great dome, constructed by Michelangelo, gives stunning vistas of Rome.

2. **Vatican Museums:** The Vatican Museums host a large collection of art, including classical statues, Renaissance masterpieces, and the world-famous Sistine Chapel. Visitors may appreciate paintings by painters including Michelangelo, Raphael, and Leonardo da Vinci.

3. **Sistine Chapel:** Located inside the Apostolic Palace, the Sistine Chapel is famed for its beautiful paintings, most notably Michelangelo's ceiling masterpiece portraying scenes from the Book of Genesis.

4. **Vatican Gardens:** These magnificently designed gardens encompass more than half of Vatican City's entire area. Visitors may discover calm walkways, fountains, and many plant marvels.

5. **Vatican Library:** The Vatican Library is one of the world's most significant study libraries, containing a massive collection of books, manuscripts, and historical documents, including notable works from antiquity.

Papal Audience & Events: Vatican City provides tourists the option to attend a Papal Audience or receive the Papal Blessing. The Papal Audience takes place on Wednesdays in St. Peter's Square or the Paul VI Audience Hall, when the Pope greets pilgrims, gives lectures and confers blessings.

Visiting Vatican City: Visitors may enter Vatican City easily from Rome. St. Peter's Square and Basilica are normally free to the public, whereas admission to the Vatican Museums requires a ticket. It is essential to reserve tickets in advance, particularly during busy tourist seasons, to prevent excessive lineups.

In conclusion, Vatican City serves as a symbol of spiritual and religious importance, drawing millions of people each year. As the spiritual seat of the Roman Catholic Church and the home of the Pope, it houses great cultural, historical, and artistic riches. From the awe-inspiring St. Peter's Basilica and the famous Vatican Museums to the tranquil Vatican Gardens, the city-state provides a multitude of experiences that make a lasting effect on those who come.

- Uffizi Gallery, Florence

The Uffizi Gallery, situated in Florence, Italy, is one of the most recognized art museums in the world. With its magnificent collection of masterpieces, historical relevance, and architectural grandeur, the Uffizi Gallery draws millions of tourists each year. Let's examine the entire content of the Uffizi Gallery, diving into its history, noteworthy artworks, architectural characteristics, and visiting experience.

1. History: The Uffizi Gallery was initially created as the administrative and judicial offices (uffizi) for the Florentine magistrates during the 16th century. The building of the Uffizi complex was begun by the Medici family, who were notable benefactors of art and culture in Florence. It was commissioned by Cosimo I de Medici and created by the great architect Giorgio Vasari.

Over the years, the structure experienced many extensions and renovations. Later, the Uffizi complex changed into a gallery when the royal house of the Medici family, notably Anna Maria Luisa de Medici, handed their large art collection to the city of Florence in 1743. This marked the founding of the Uffizi Gallery as a public institution.

2. Architectural Features: The Uffizi Gallery features an amazing architectural design. The structure follows a U-shaped form, around a wide courtyard known as the Piazza della Signoria. The front has a beautiful blend of Renaissance and Mannerist architectural elements, marked by a rhythm of arches, pilasters, and windows.

The Vasari Corridor, an elevated walkway, links the Uffizi Gallery with the Pitti Palace, another notable Medici palace. This corridor extends over the Ponte Vecchio, a historic footbridge that overlooks the Arno River. The Vasari Corridor also includes a huge collection of portraits of himself, including works by painters like Rembrandt and Velázquez.

3. Notable Artworks: The Uffizi Gallery holds an outstanding collection of artworks, encompassing a broad variety of eras and creative styles. Some of the most notable works include:
- "The Birth of Venus" and "Primavera" by Sandro Botticelli - "Annunciation" by Leonardo da Vinci - "Madonna and Child with Two Angels" by Filippo Lippi - "Doni Tondo" by Michelangelo - "Venus of Urbino" by Titian - "Adoration of the Magi" by Gentile da Fabriano - "Bacchus" and "Medusa" by Caravaggio - "Judith Slaying Holofernes" by Artemisia Gentileschi. These are only a few samples from the huge collection of paintings, sculptures, and decorative arts shown at the museum.

4. Visitor Experience:
The Uffizi Gallery provides an exciting and engaging experience for art fans and visitors

alike. When visiting the gallery, it is important to plan owing to its popularity and large visitor numbers. Here are a few recommendations to improve your visit:

- **Tickets**: To prevent excessive lineups, it is advisable to reserve tickets in advance. Online bookings or buying a timed-entry ticket can save you time and guarantee quick access to the museum.

- **Guided Tours**: Engaging a professional guide or taking a guided tour will substantially increase your knowledge and enjoyment of the artwork. Guides give vital insights, historical background, and stories about the artists and their works.

- **Must-view Artworks**: Due to the vast amount of artwork, it might be hard to view everything in one visit. Prioritize the must-see masterpieces, and organize your trip accordingly. A map or audio tour may aid in exploring the gallery.

- **Time of Visit**: Consider going during the calmer hours, such as early morning or late afternoon, to avoid crowds and get a more personal encounter with the art.

- **Facilities**: The Uffizi Gallery includes services including toilets, a bookshop, and a café. Take breaks, sip refreshments, and browse the gift store for art-related items and literature.

5. Impact and Legacy: The Uffizi Gallery contains tremendous cultural and historical value. It embodies the aesthetic and intellectual heritage of Florence, a city famed for its contribution to the Renaissance. The Medici family's sponsorship of the arts and their preservation of major artworks had a key part in developing the gallery's collection.

Moreover, the Uffizi Gallery has influenced several art museums worldwide, acting as a model for showing and conserving art. Its influence goes beyond its doors, touching the art world and creating a better appreciation for Italian Renaissance art.

In conclusion, the Uffizi Gallery serves as a tribute to Florence's rich cultural past and the Medici family's sponsorship of the arts. Its extraordinary collection, majestic building, and compelling ambiance make it a must-visit site for art aficionados and history enthusiasts. Exploring the Uffizi Gallery invites visitors to immerse themselves in the beauty and ingenuity of some of the most outstanding artworks ever produced.

- St. Mark's Square, Venice

St. Mark's Plaza, known as Piazza San Marco in Italian, is the major public plaza in Venice, Italy. This renowned and historic plaza is not just the center of the city but also a dynamic center of activity, culture, and architectural beauty. Let's go into the complete material of St. Mark's Square, covering its history, noteworthy monuments, distinctive characteristics, and visiting experience.

1. History: St. Mark's Square has a rich and legendary history that reaches back to the 9th century. Originally, it functioned as a modest public plaza in front of St. Mark's Basilica, which was the chapel of the Doge's Palace. Over time, as Venice developed in power and prominence, the plaza expanded and became a significant meeting place for political, religious, and social activity.

2. Landmarks: St. Mark's Square is recognized for its stunning architectural features, each reflecting a distinct period and style. Here are some prominent landmarks inside the square:

- **St. Mark's Basilica**: The spectacular Byzantine-style basilica dominates the eastern end of the plaza. Adorned with beautiful mosaics, marble columns, and decorative domes, the basilica is a magnificent marvel of architecture.

- **Doge's Palace**: Adjacent to the church, the Doge's Palace stands as a symbol of Venetian political authority. This Gothic palace served as the home of the Doge (ruler of Venice) and housed administrative offices. It boasts stunning courtyards, great rooms, and a famed Bridge of Sighs.

- **Campanile di San Marco**: The lofty bell tower, situated near the entrance of the plaza, gives panoramic views of Venice. Rebuilt in the 20th century, it mimics the old 16th-century campanile that fell in 1902.

- **Procuratie structures**: These arcaded structures border the plaza and were formerly inhabited by the offices of the Procurators, administrators of the Republic of Venice. Today, they hold upscale stores, cafés, and museums.

- **Clock Tower**: Standing near the entrance to the Mercerie commercial strip, the Clock Tower is an attractive Renaissance edifice. Its clock mechanism, with its bronze sculptures and moving figures, is an amazing sight to see.

3. distinctive elements: St. Mark's Square possesses various distinctive elements that contribute to its allure:

- **Pigeons**: The plaza is noted for its vast population of pigeons, who have become an unofficial emblem of the area. Feeding the pigeons has long been a favorite pastime for guests, providing a vibrant and unique ambiance.

- **Flooding**: St. Mark's Square is prone to occasional flooding, known as "aqua alta," produced by the rising waters of the lagoon. Elevated walkways dubbed "acqua alta" platforms are put in place during these episodes to guarantee people can still reach the area.

4. Visitor Experience: St. Mark's Square delivers a wonderful experience for tourists. Here are some recommendations to make the most of your visit:

- **Timing**: Consider going early in the morning or late in the evening to avoid crowds and enjoy a more serene experience. Strolling in the area after sunset or at night may be very lovely.

- **Tour the sites**: Take the opportunity to tour the numerous sites surrounding the plaza, including the church, the Doge's Palace, and the bell tower. Inside each of these sites, you'll encounter incredible architecture, art, and historical treasures.

- **Outdoor cafés**: Relax and absorb the ambiance of the plaza by sitting at one of the outdoor cafés. Enjoy a cup of coffee or a typical Venetian spritz while taking in the sights and people-watching.

- **Live Music**: St. Mark's Square regularly has live music performances, offering a lovely accompaniment to your stay. Classical orchestras, bands, and street entertainers add to the dynamic atmosphere.

- **Evening Illumination**: Witness the square's metamorphosis at night when the buildings are magnificently lighted, creating a romantic and fascinating ambiance.

5. Cultural importance: St. Mark's Square possesses enormous cultural importance for the people of Venice. It serves as a gathering place, a site for festivities and festivals, and a symbol of the city's grandeur and history. The square has been an inspiration for innumerable painters, poets, and singers over the years, immortalizing its beauty in different creative forms.

In conclusion, St. Mark's Square is a mesmerizing place that encompasses the spirit of Venice. Its historic monuments, architectural magnificence, dynamic atmosphere, and cultural relevance make it an unmissable aspect of any visit to the city. By wandering St. Mark's Square, tourists may immerse themselves in the timeless elegance and rich tradition of Venice.

- Duomo di Milano, Milan

The Duomo di Milano, often known as the Milan Cathedral, is one of the most famous monuments in the city of Milan, Italy. This majestic cathedral is a marvel of Gothic architecture and serves as a tribute to the rich cultural legacy of the area. With its exquisite features, soaring spires, and magnificent façade, the Duomo di Milano draws millions of people from across the globe each year.

Construction of the Duomo di Milano started in 1386 and took over six decades to finish. The cathedral was erected on the site of a medieval basilica and was meant to be a majestic emblem of Milan's riches and power. The major architect responsible for the original design was Simone da Orsenigo, although, throughout the years, various other architects made important contributions to the construction.

One of the most outstanding elements of the Duomo di Milano is its façade. Made entirely of Candoglia marble, the exquisite workmanship, and rich ornamentation are simply awe-inspiring. The façade is ornamented with innumerable sculptures, including various saints, angels, and gargoyles. The central spire, known as the Madonnina, is capped with a figure of the Virgin Mary, which has become one of Milan's most famous emblems.

The inside of the cathedral is similarly gorgeous. Upon entering, guests are overwhelmed with an overpowering feeling of grandeur. The nave is over 150 meters long, and its ornate stone columns support the spectacular domed roof. The stained glass windows, dating back to the 15th century, enable soft, multicolored light to pervade the chamber, creating a tranquil and ethereal mood.

One of the features of the Duomo di Milano is the rooftop terrace, which gives stunning panoramic views of the city. Accessible by steps or an elevator, tourists may examine the beautifully carved spires and pinnacles up close. Walking up the rooftop, one can see the painstaking workmanship and attention to detail that went into producing this architectural wonder.

The Duomo di Milano is also home to several items of art and historical artifacts. The cathedral has a treasure where visitors may examine a variety of priceless objects, including tapestries, holy utensils, and liturgical costumes. The Archaeological Area, situated underneath the cathedral, shows the remnants of the ancient Baptistery of San Giovanni alle Fonti and the Basilica of Santa Tecla.

In addition to its architectural and aesthetic importance, the Duomo di Milano plays an important role in the religious and cultural life of Milan. It is the seat of the Archbishop of Milan and remains an active place of worship. The cathedral holds religious rituals, concerts, and other cultural events throughout the year, drawing both residents and visitors.

Visiting the Duomo di Milano is a must for anybody visiting Milan. Its sheer grandeur and beauty create a lasting impact, and the option to explore the rooftop terrace is a unique experience. Whether you are interested in history, or architecture, or just seeking a moment of serenity in the center of the busy city, the Duomo di Milano provides a mesmerizing voyage through time and craftsmanship.

- Pompeii

Pompeii is an ancient Roman city situated near contemporary times Naples in Italy. It is internationally famous for its sad and interesting past, as well as its wonderfully maintained ruins. Pompeii was once a bustling and rich city until its terrible destruction by the eruption of Mount Vesuvius in 79 AD. Today, it stands as an archaeological site of tremendous historical and cultural value, drawing millions of tourists each year.

1. **Historical Background**: Pompeii was established in the 6th century BC by the Oscan people, an old Italic tribe. It gradually fell under Greek influence and finally became a Roman

colony around 80 BC. The city developed during Roman authority, functioning as a significant hub for trade, commerce, and agriculture. Pompeii's advantageous position near the Bay of Naples made it a busy center of activity and attracted a varied population.

2. **Mount Vesuvius Eruption**: The eruption of Mount Vesuvius on August 24, 79 AD, is one of the most well-known natural catastrophes in history. The eruption buried Pompeii and numerous other adjacent villages beneath a thick layer of volcanic ash and pumice. The city was overwhelmed by a pyroclastic surge, which instantaneously killed thousands of individuals and preserved the city beneath layers of volcanic debris.

3. **Rediscovery and Excavation**: Pompeii remains buried and mostly forgotten until its rediscovery in the 18th century. Excavations, first directed by the Spanish military engineer Rocque Joaquin de Alcubierre in 1748, uncovered a surprisingly well-preserved picture of ancient Roman society. The site continues to be intensively dug until this day, with continued attempts to unearth and protect its riches.

4. **Architecture and Urban Planning**: Pompeii's architecture exhibits the creativity and skill of the ancient Romans. The city included great houses, public buildings, temples, theaters, and a complex network of streets and lanes. The architectural styles varied from modest and efficient to extravagant and sumptuous. Notable constructions include the Forum, the Amphitheater, the Temple of Apollo, and the House of the Faun.

5. **Everyday Life in Pompeii**: The archaeological remains of Pompeii give a wonderful glimpse into the everyday life of its residents. The city had a complicated social structure, including affluent patricians, merchants, freedmen, and slaves. Pompeii had many stores, pubs, and markets, suggesting a lively economy. The remains also give data about the Roman diet, bathing habits, entertainment, and religious traditions.

6. **Art and Culture**: Pompeii was a hotbed of artistic and cultural activity. The walls of numerous buildings are covered with magnificent paintings representing scenes from mythology, landscapes, and daily life. Intricate mosaics graced the floors of aristocratic residences, while sculptures and statues

ornamented public areas. The city also had a well-established theatrical culture, and evidence of plays and performances has been uncovered.

7. **Preservation and Conservation**: The volcanic ash and debris that buried Pompeii worked as a protective covering, protecting buildings, objects, and even human remains. Excavations have unearthed exceptionally well-preserved buildings, frescoes, graffiti, and daily things. However, vulnerability to weather and a growing number of tourists have created problems for the site's protection. Conservation works are undertaken to safeguard the long-term preservation of the ruins.

8. **Tourism and Cultural Significance**: Pompeii is a UNESCO World Heritage site and draws millions of tourists each year. It gives a rare chance to witness an ancient Roman city preserved in time. The site gives unique insights into ancient Roman civilization, urban planning, architecture, and everyday life. Pompeii serves as a sad reminder of the destructive force of nature and the ephemeral character of human existence.

In conclusion, Pompeii exists as a magnificent archaeological site that gives an insight into the everyday life of ancient Romans. Its terrible demolition and subsequent restoration have given it a priceless window into the past. Pompeii's remains continue to attract tourists, historians, and archaeologists alike, affording a physical link to the ancient world and offering significant insights into the depth of human history and cultural legacy.

- Mount Vesuvius

Mount Vesuvius is one of the most renowned and active volcanoes in the world. It is situated on the western coast of Italy, between the towns of Naples and Pompeii. With a height of about 4,203 feet (1,281 meters), Mount Vesuvius dominates the skyline of the area and has had a vital influence in defining its history, geology, and cultural legacy.

1. **Geographical and Geological Background**: Mount Vesuvius is part of the Campanian volcanic arc, which spans along the western coast of Italy. It is classed as a stratovolcano, sometimes known as a composite volcano, distinguished by its steep slopes and explosive eruptions. The volcano is located inside the broader Vesuvius National Park, which includes an area of around 85 square kilometers.

2. **Historical Eruptions**: Mount Vesuvius is infamous for its cataclysmic eruption in 79 AD, which buried the towns of Pompeii, Herculaneum, and Stabiae beneath masses of volcanic ash and pumice. The eruption was a pyroclastic surge, unleashing a large column of gas, ash, and boulders that reached an estimated height of 21 miles (33 kilometers). It caused the fast death of thousands of people and preserved the towns under the ash, offering a unique glimpse of ancient Roman life.

Vesuvius has experienced multiple eruptions since then, with noteworthy occurrences happening in 1631, 1794, 1906, and 1944. The eruption in 1631 was exceptionally disastrous, resulting in the loss of thousands of lives and the ruin of countless settlements. The volcano has been inactive since its last eruption in 1944, although it is still considered an active volcano with the potential for future eruptions.

3. **Impact on Pompeii and Herculaneum**: The eruption of Mount Vesuvius in 79 AD had a major impact on the adjacent towns of Pompeii and Herculaneum. The sudden burial of these settlements beneath volcanic ash and debris preserved them exceptionally well, offering archaeologists important insights into ancient

Roman culture, architecture, and daily life. Excavations in Pompeii and Herculaneum have discovered well-preserved structures, frescoes, mosaics, and artifacts, shedding light on numerous facets of Roman civilization.

4. **Volcanic threats and Monitoring**: The volcanic activity of Mount Vesuvius creates potential threats to the surrounding area. These risks include pyroclastic flows, volcanic ash, lava flows, and volcanic gases. As a consequence, comprehensive monitoring systems are in place to analyze volcanic activity and offer early warnings to neighboring people. The National Institute of Geophysics and Volcanology (INGV) regularly monitors Vesuvius using seismometers, gas analyzers, and other sensors to identify any symptoms of volcanic disturbance.

5. **Tourism and Cultural Significance**: Mount Vesuvius and its related ancient monuments, notably Pompeii and Herculaneum, draw millions of visitors each year. Visitors have the chance to trek to the crater of Vesuvius, affording panoramic views of the surrounding area. The archaeological sites give a rare opportunity to study the old Roman settlements that were preserved by the volcano's explosion.

These places are of tremendous cultural value, enabling visitors to immerse themselves in the everyday life, art, and architecture of the Roman period.

6. **Environmental Importance**: Apart from its historical and cultural value, Mount Vesuvius also bears environmental importance. The volcanic soils around the volcano are rich and sustain agricultural activity, notably the production of grapes for the famed wines of the area. The Vesuvius National Park is home to rich flora and animals, including rare and unique species that have adapted to the volcanic environment.

In conclusion, Mount Vesuvius is a spectacular and famous volcano with a rich history and cultural heritage. Its eruptions have changed the environment, impacted the fate of adjacent communities, and offered significant archaeological insights into ancient Roman civilization. With continued monitoring efforts and responsible tourism, Mount Vesuvius remains to be a mesmerizing and recognized natural beauty.

- Capri Island

Capri Island, situated in the Tyrrhenian Sea off the coast of Naples, Italy, is a scenic and charming place that has grabbed the hearts of tourists for ages. With its spectacular natural beauty, dynamic culture, and historical importance, Capri has become a desired holiday location and a symbol of Mediterranean elegance. Let's explore this beautiful island in greater depth.

Geography and Location: Capri is a tiny Italian island covering around 10 square kilometers (4 square miles) in size. It is part of the Campania area and falls inside the broader Bay of Naples. The island is defined by its rough shoreline, towering cliffs, and stunning rock formations, especially the famed Faraglioni rocks that protrude out of the turquoise water. The highest point on the island is Monte Solaro, reaching a height of 589 meters (1,932 feet), affording amazing panoramic views of the surrounding region.

Natural Beauty: The natural beauty of Capri is outstanding and has captivated travelers for years. From the craggy shoreline to the lush greenery, the island provides a broad spectrum of vistas. The Blue Grotto (Grotta Azzurra) is one of Capri's most renowned natural attractions. Visitors may take a boat trip and enter the cave, where sunlight pouring through an underwater chamber lights the water, producing a beautiful blue glow.

Another important natural attraction is the Gardens of Augustus (Giardini di Augusto), situated in the town of Capri. These magnificent gardens give breathtaking views of the Faraglioni cliffs and provide a calm respite among bright flowers and Mediterranean plants.

Sites and Attractions: Capri is recognized for its variety of sites and attractions that exhibit its rich history and cultural heritage. The town of Capri is a buzzing metropolis with upscale stores, attractive cafés, and exquisite homes. The Piazzetta, commonly referred to as the "living room of the world," is the primary area where people and tourists meet to interact and enjoy the bustling environment.

Villa Jovis, positioned on the eastern cliffs of the island, was erected by Emperor Tiberius in the 1st century AD and served as his imperial home. Today, tourists may explore the remains and marvel at the beautiful vistas of the Gulf of Naples.

Anacapri, the second biggest town on the island, provides its collection of attractions. The chairlift to Monte Solaro delivers a wonderful journey to the peak, enabling guests to take in the panoramic sights. Additionally, the Church of San Michele is a must-visit attraction, noted for its majolica-tiled floor representing the expulsion of Adam and Eve from the Garden of Eden.

Cultural Significance: Capri has been a source of inspiration for painters, authors, and philosophers throughout history. It has acted as an inspiration for prominent personalities including Pablo Neruda, Graham Greene, and Axel Munthe. The island's appeal and beauty have also captured famous historical characters, like Emperor Augustus, who made Capri his secret hideaway.

The island's attraction continues to entice celebrities and jet-setters, who enjoy its exclusivity and refined ambiance. From gorgeous hotels and fancy restaurants to high-end shopping, Capri is a playground for the affluent and famous.

Local Cuisine: Capri's culinary scene is a fascinating blend of classic Italian tastes and fresh Mediterranean ingredients. Seafood is a feature, with dishes like spaghetti alle vongole (spaghetti with clams) and puzzolana all'acqua pizza (sea bream in crazy water) being local favorites. Visitors may also sample the island's famed limoncello, a lemon liqueur created from the aromatic lemons growing in the area.

Outdoor Activities: In addition to its natural and cultural charms, Capri provides a selection of outdoor activities for adventure seekers. Hiking routes traverse the island, enabling tourists to experience its stunning splendor on foot. The Via Krupp, an ancient cliffside walk, provides stunning vistas as it snakes its way down to the Marina Piccola.

Boat trips are a popular method to explore the island's secret coves and grottoes while swimming and snorkeling in the crystal-clear waters of the Mediterranean are a refreshing way to experience the island's coastline splendor.

In conclusion, Capri Island's blend of natural beauty, historical sites, and active culture make it a wonderful trip. Whether you are seeking a luxury holiday, an investigation of ancient history, or just a chance to immerse yourself in the gorgeous scenery, Capri has something to offer every tourist. With its magical attractiveness and ageless appeal, Capri remains to be a mesmerizing treasure in the Mediterranean.

- Leaning Tower of Pisa

The Leaning Tower of Pisa, known as "Torre Pendente di Pisa" in Italian, is one of the most recognized architectural buildings in the world. Located in the city of Pisa, Italy, this magnificent tower has fascinated tourists for ages with its characteristic lean and unique beauty. Here is a thorough review of the Leaning Tower of Pisa, encompassing its history, architectural elements, importance, and tourist draw.

History:
The building of the Leaning Tower of Pisa started in 1173 and proceeded for approximately 200 years. It was initially meant to be a standalone bell tower for the adjacent Pisa Cathedral. However, the tower began to tilt during its construction owing to unstable

subsurface made of soft clay, sand, and water. This led the tower to lean towards the south.

Construction was interrupted multiple times due to political upheavals and wars, enabling the earth to settle. The tower's lean was partly straightened during these breaks, although it remained inclined. Despite attempts to stabilize the structure, the tilt continued to rise throughout the years.

Architectural Features:

The Leaning Tower of Pisa rises at a height of roughly 55.86 meters (183.27 feet) on its tallest side and 56.70 meters (186.02 feet) on its lowest side. It consists of eight levels, including the bell chamber at the top. The tower is made of white marble and has Romanesque architectural elements.

The tower's lean is the consequence of the unequal distribution of weight and the sinking of the soft ground on its southern side. At its most severe, the top of the tower leans at an angle of around 5.5 degrees from the vertical. However, major repair and stability operations have decreased the lean to a safer degree, making it accessible to tourists.

Significance:

The Leaning Tower of Pisa is not merely an architectural masterpiece; it also carries immense historical and cultural value. It serves as a symbol of the city of Pisa and depicts the richness and power the city once held throughout the medieval era. The tower, together with the Pisa Cathedral and the Baptistery of Pisa, constitutes the Piazza dei Miracoli (Square of Miracles), a UNESCO World Heritage Site.

The tower's unusual tilt has also become an iconic feature of Pisa, drawing millions of visitors from across the globe. It has been represented in many images, paintings, and works of literature, confirming its reputation as a worldwide symbol.

Tourist Attraction:

The Leaning Tower of Pisa is a prominent tourist attraction, bringing people who are attracted by its fascinating lean and architectural grandeur. Climbing to the top of the tower is a popular pastime, affording panoramic views over the city of Pisa and its environs. However, because of safety concerns, there are limitations on the number of guests permitted inside at a time.

In addition to the tower, the Piazza dei Miracoli has several important sights. The Pisa Cathedral, with its spectacular architecture and rich interiors, is a must-visit. The Baptistery, a circular marble monument, is recognized for its remarkable acoustics. The Camposanto Monumentale, a monumental cemetery, also contributes to the historical and cultural richness of the region.

To maintain and sustain the tower, numerous repair works have been carried out throughout the years. In 2001, the tower was reopened to the public following a decade-long rehabilitation process that effectively decreased its tilt.

In conclusion, the Leaning Tower of Pisa remains a tribute to human ingenuity, as it continues to defy gravity and grab the imagination of people worldwide. Its bending structure, rich history, and architectural magnificence make it a fascinating landmark. Visiting the Leaning Tower of Pisa gives you a rare chance to view this astounding feat of engineering and enjoy the continuing fascination of this renowned Italian monument.

- Lake Como

Lake Como, situated in the Lombardy area of northern Italy, is one of the most beautiful and known lakes in the nation. It is famed for its outstanding natural beauty, lovely lakeside villages, exquisite mansions, and stunning alpine vistas. Lake Como has been a famous destination for decades, drawing people from all over the globe who come to enjoy its gorgeous scenery and elegant ambiance. Here is a thorough description of Lake Como, including its topography, attractions, activities, and history.

Geography and Location:

Lake Como, or Lago di Bellagio in Italian, is a glacial lake located at the Italian Alpine. It is the third-biggest lake in Italy, with an area of around 146 square kilometers (56 square miles). The lake has a characteristic "Y" form, with the town of Como lying at the southwestern tip, the town of Lecco at the southeastern tip, and the town of Colico at the northernmost point. The lake is surrounded by rugged hills and mountains, providing a dramatic and scenic environment.

Towns and Villages:

Lake Como is filled with lovely cities and villages that provide a unique combination of history, culture, and natural beauty. Some of the more significant settlements around the lake include:

1. **Como**: Situated at the southwestern edge, Como is the biggest town on Lake Como and acts as a gateway to the lake. It has a lovely old town with small streets, antique buildings, and a magnificent lakeside promenade.

2. **Bellagio**: Often referred to as the "Pearl of Lake Como," Bellagio is a lovely hamlet situated at the junction of the lake's three branches. It is recognized for its exquisite houses, lovely gardens, and panoramic vistas.

3. **Varenna**: Nestled on the eastern coast of the lake, Varenna is a picturesque and tiny hamlet with colorful buildings, narrow lanes, and a charming beachfront. It provides spectacular views of the lake and is a favorite location for couples and nature lovers.

4. **Menaggio**: Located on the western coast, Menaggio is a vibrant town famed for its attractive plaza, lakeside promenade, and stunning public gardens. It is a popular location for visiting the center region of Lake Como.

5. **Tremezzo**: Situated on the western coast, Tremezzo is noted for its stately homes and luxurious hotels. The most noteworthy sight in Tremezzo is mansion Carlotta, a lovely mansion with exquisite gardens overlooking the lake.

Attractions and Activities:

Lake Como provides a broad selection of sights and activities to satisfy every taste. Here are some of the highlights:

1. **Estate del Balbianello**: Situated on a promontory near Lenno, Estate del Balbianello is a lovely estate with terraced gardens that give stunning views of the lake. The villa has been featured in various movies, including "Casino Royale" and "Star Wars: Episode II - Attack of the Clones."

2. **Palace Carlotta**: Located in Tremezzo, Palace Carlotta is a neoclassical palace famed for its art collection and exquisite floral gardens. Visitors may explore the villa's sumptuous chambers and wander around the wonderfully planted grounds.

3. **Boat rides**: One of the finest ways to explore Lake Como is by taking a boat trip. The boat service links numerous villages surrounding the lake, enabling guests to enjoy the picturesque views and bounce between different attractions.

4. **Water sports**: Lake Como provides lots of chances for water sports aficionados. Sailing, windsurfing, kayaking, and paddleboarding are popular sports on the lake. Rental services and courses are available for people seeking to attempt these hobbies.

5. **Trekking and nature walk**: The neighboring mountains give good chances for trekking and nature walks. Numerous pathways give spectacular views of the lake and the surrounding mountain environment. The Greenway del Lago di Como, a 10-kilometer-long picturesque route, is a favorite option among hikers.

History and Culture:

Lake Como has a rich history that reaches back to prehistoric times. The territory was inhabited by Celtic tribes before it fell under Roman domination in the 2nd century BC. Throughout history, Lake Como has been a popular refuge for the affluent and aristocracy, who erected exquisite palaces and gardens along its shores.

The lake also retains cultural value, since it has inspired numerous painters, authors, and musicians throughout the years. Famous musician Franz Liszt, for example, stayed at the Villa d'Este at Cernobbio, while famous writer

Alessandro Manzoni, who based part of his book "The Betrothed" on the beaches of Lake Como.

In conclusion, lake Como's natural beauty, quaint cities, and cultural legacy make it a delightful trip. Whether you're seeking leisure, outdoor activities, or a taste of history and culture, Lake Como provides a plethora of experiences. With its breathtaking vistas, exquisite houses, and tranquil ambiance, Lake Como continues to enchant tourists and remains a treasure of northern Italy.

CHAPTER 5. Experiencing Italian Cuisine

- Regional Italian Cuisine

Italy, famed for its rich culinary past, is a treasure trove of regional cuisines. The country's culinary scene is as varied as its culture and geography. From the northern alpine areas to the sun-drenched islands in the south, each location of Italy has its distinct culinary traditions and local ingredients. Exploring regional Italian food is like starting on a wonderful trip across the country's unique tastes and culinary cultures.

1. **Northern Italian Cuisine**: Northern Italy is recognized for its substantial and sophisticated recipes that typically contain ingredients like rice, polenta, butter, and cream. Lombardy, Piedmont, and Emilia-Romagna are the important regions in this area.

- **Lombardy**: Famous for its creamy risottos, notably the famous saffron-infused Risotto alla Milanese. Another Lombardian specialty is ossobuco, a cooked veal shank dish. The area is also famed for its creamy cheeses like Gorgonzola and Taleggio.

- **Piedmont**: Renowned for its truffles, Piedmont provides delicacies like Tajarin, a pasta cooked with a large number of egg yolks, sometimes topped with shaved truffles. The area is also the origin of the renowned beef dish, Bollito Misto, and the exquisite dessert, gianduja chocolate.

- **Emilia-Romagna**: Home to renowned towns like Bologna and Parma, Emilia-Romagna is famed for its pasta dishes, such as lasagna, tortellini, and tagliatelle. Parmigiano Reggiano cheese, prosciutto di Parma, and balsamic vinegar from Modena are further highlights of this area.

2. **Central Italian Cuisine**: Central Italy is noted for its rustic and simple but tasty cuisine, typically emphasizing fresh ingredients. The areas of Tuscany, Umbria, and Lazio are notable gastronomic attractions in this area.

- **Tuscany**: Tuscany is known for its farm-to-table mentality, with delicacies like Ribollita (a hearty vegetable and bread soup), Bistecca alla Fiorentina (a thick-cut T-bone steak), and Pappa al Pomodoro (a tomato and bread soup). The area is particularly recognized for its powerful red wines, such as Chianti and Brunello di Montalcino.

- **Umbria**: Known as the "green heart" of Italy, Umbria offers foods like Porchetta (roast pig seasoned with herbs), Strangozzi (a sort of pasta commonly eaten with truffles), and Norcia-style cured meats. The region's lentils from Castelluccio and the superb chocolate of Perugia are highly acclaimed.

- **Lazio**: Lazio is home to Rome, where traditional foods like Carbonara (pasta with egg, pecorino cheese, and pancetta), Cacio e Pepe (pasta with pecorino cheese and black pepper), and Saltimbocca alla Romana (veal wrapped in prosciutto and sage) originated. The area is also famed for its artichokes, notably the Roman-style carciofi alla giudia.

3. **Southern Italian Cuisine**: Southern Italian cuisine displays the bright tastes of the Mediterranean, with a focus on fresh seafood, sun-ripened vegetables, and powerful spices. The areas of Campania, Sicily, and Puglia are gastronomic wonders in the south.

- **Campania**: Known for the classic Neapolitan pizza, Campania provides additional treats like Pasta e Fagioli (pasta with beans), Mozzarella di Bufala (buffalo mozzarella), and Eggplant Parmigiana. The area is also home to the renowned limoncello liqueur, manufactured from Amalfi Coast lemons.

- **Sicily**: Influenced by numerous Mediterranean civilizations, Sicilian food is a mix of tastes. Arancini (fried rice balls), Caponata (a sweet and sour eggplant relish), and Pasta alla Norma (pasta with tomatoes, eggplant, and ricotta salata) are just a few of the island's signature meals. Sicily is also noted for its seafood, cannoli, and Marsala wine.

- **Puglia**: Located in the "heel" of Italy, Puglia is noted for its basic and nutritious food. Orecchiette (ear-shaped pasta), Burrata cheese, Focaccia Barese, and Taralli (savory biscuits) are among the region's gastronomic specialties. Puglia is also a large producer of olive oil.

4. **Island Cuisine**: Italy's islands have their culinary traditions, formed by their distinctive geographical settings and cultural influences.

- **Sardinia**: Sardinian cuisine is renowned for its rustic and substantial meals. Roast suckling pig (porceddu), Malloreddus (Sardinian gnocchi), and Pane Carasau (crispy flatbread) are Sardinian delicacies. The island also features wonderful sheep's milk cheeses like Pecorino Sardo.

- **Sicily**: As indicated before, Sicilian food provides a richness of tastes, integrating influences from Arab, Greek, and Norman civilizations. Alongside its classic cuisine, the island is famed for its sweet delicacies like Cassata (ricotta-stuffed cake) and Cannoli (fried pastry tubes filled with sweet ricotta).

Exploring regional Italian cuisine is a fascinating way to appreciate the country's gastronomic variety and relish the particular flavors of each area. Whether you're indulging in the creamy risottos of the north, the simple elegance of central Italian meals, the Mediterranean pleasures of the south, or the island delicacies, Italy's regional cuisine offers a gourmet trip that will leave you hungry for more. Buon appetito!

- Popular Italian Dishes

Italian cuisine is renowned worldwide for its rich flavors, fresh ingredients, and culinary traditions. From pasta and pizza to gelato and tiramisu, Italian cuisine offers a delightful range of dishes that have become popular globally. In this comprehensive guide, we will explore some of the most beloved and iconic Italian dishes.

1. **Pasta Carbonara**: Pasta Carbonara is a classic Roman dish that combines pasta with a creamy sauce made from eggs, Pecorino Romano cheese, pancetta or guanciale (Italian cured pork jowl), and black pepper. The result is a rich and indulgent dish with a perfect balance of flavors.

2. **Margherita Pizza**: Considered the mother of all pizzas, Margherita Pizza is a simple yet delicious creation that originated in Naples. It features a thin crust topped with fresh tomato sauce, mozzarella cheese, and basil leaves. The combination of these basic ingredients creates a harmonious blend of flavors that represents the colors of the Italian flag.

3. **Lasagna**: Lasagna is a comforting baked pasta dish made with layers of lasagna noodles, rich meat sauce, béchamel sauce, and cheese. It is often enhanced with ingredients like ground beef, Italian sausage, mushrooms, and various herbs. The result is a hearty and satisfying dish that is perfect for gatherings and special occasions.

4. **Risotto alla Milanese**: Risotto alla Milanese is a creamy and aromatic rice dish hailing from the city of Milan. It is prepared by cooking Arborio or Carnaroli rice with saffron, butter,

onion, white wine, and Parmesan cheese. The finished dish has a vibrant yellow color and a rich, velvety texture.

5. **Bruschetta**: Bruschetta is a popular Italian appetizer that consists of grilled bread rubbed with garlic, topped with ripe tomatoes, fresh basil, extra-virgin olive oil, and a sprinkle of salt. It's a simple dish that highlights the freshness and quality of the ingredients.

6. **Tiramisu**: Tiramisu is a classic Italian dessert that translates to "pick me up" in Italian, thanks to its coffee-infused flavors. This luscious dessert is made with ladyfingers dipped in coffee, layered with a creamy mixture of mascarpone cheese, eggs, and sugar, and dusted with cocoa powder. Tiramisu is a beloved sweet treat that is indulgent and irresistible.

7. **Pizza Napoletana**: Originating from Naples, Pizza Napoletana is a style of pizza that adheres to strict traditional standards. It features a soft and chewy crust with a raised edge, topped with San Marzano tomatoes, buffalo mozzarella cheese, fresh basil, and extra-virgin olive oil. It is cooked in a wood-fired oven at high temperatures, resulting in a pizza with a charred, flavorful crust.

8. **Osso Buco**: Osso Buco is a delicious Milanese specialty made from braised veal shanks. The shanks are slowly cooked in a flavorful broth with vegetables, white wine, and herbs until the meat becomes tender and succulent. It is often served with a gremolata (a mixture of lemon zest, garlic, and parsley) and enjoyed with risotto.

9. **Gelato**: Gelato, the Italian version of ice cream, is known for its dense, creamy texture and intense flavors. It is made with milk, sugar, and various flavorings such as fruits, nuts, chocolate, or coffee. Unlike traditional ice cream, gelato contains less fat and less air, resulting in a denser and more flavorful frozen treat.

10. **Ossobuco**: Ossobuco is a traditional Italian dish made with braised veal shanks cooked in a flavorful broth.

- Wine and Food Pairings

Wine and food pairings are an integral aspect of Italian cuisine, which is famous worldwide for its rich tastes and unique regional specialties. With a lengthy history of winemaking and a diverse variety of grape varietals, Italy provides a large assortment of wines that may perfectly match its traditional culinary pleasures. In this thorough guide, we will study the art of wine and food pairings in Italy, taking into account the country's various regional cuisine and the characteristics of its popular wines.

1. **Understanding Italian Wine Regions**: Italy is split into 20 wine regions, each with its particular wine styles and grape varieties. Some of the well-known wine areas include Tuscany, Piedmont, Veneto, Sicily, and Friuli-Venezia Giulia. It's crucial to learn the traits and tastes associated with each location to make smart wine-matching decisions.

2. **Key Italian Grape types**: Italy possesses an incredible assortment of indigenous grape types, delivering a diverse range of tastes, aromas, and characteristics. Some of the major grape varietals to be acquainted with are Sangiovese, Nebbiolo, Barbera, Montepulciano, Primitivo, Nero d'Avola, Trebbiano, Verdicchio, and Garganega, among many more. Each grape type adds to the particular taste characteristics of Italian wines.

3. **Wine and Food mixing principles**: When it comes to mixing Italian wines with food, there are certain fundamental principles to bear in

mind. However, personal tastes and geographical variances in food may impact your selections. Here are some recommendations to help you get started:

a. **Red Wines: - Sangiovese**: This adaptable grape type provides the backbone of many renowned Tuscan wines, such as Chianti and Brunello di Montalcino. Sangiovese works nicely with tomato-based pasta dishes, roasted meats, and aged cheeses.

- **Nebbiolo**: Known for creating elegant and tannic wines like Barolo and Barbaresco, Nebbiolo works nicely with substantial foods like braised meats, truffles, and aged cheeses.

b. **White Wines: - Verdicchio**: A crisp and refreshing white wine from the Marche area, Verdicchio works nicely with seafood, shellfish, and light pasta dishes.

- **Gavi**: Made from the Cortese grape in Piedmont, Gavi is a dry white wine that compliments seafood, vegetable risottos, and fresh cheeses.

c. **Sparkling Wines: - Prosecco**: This light and fruity sparkling wine from the Veneto area goes nicely with appetizers, light fish dishes, and fresh fruit.

- **Franciacorta**: Known as the Italian Champagne, Franciacorta is a high-quality sparkling wine that can be combined with a range of foods, including seafood, chicken, and delicate sweets.

d. **Sweet Wines: - Moscato d'Asti**: A delicious, low-alcohol sparkling wine with flowery and fruity notes, Moscato d'Asti is a fantastic complement with fruit-based sweets, pastries, and mild cheeses.

- **Vin Santo**: A typical Tuscan dessert wine, Vin Santo goes nicely with biscotti, almond-based pastries, and aged cheeses.

4. **Regional Pairing Recommendations**: Italian food is very varied, with each area claiming its own peculiarities and culinary traditions. Here are some geographical matching tips to improve your dining experience:

- **Tuscany**: Pair a classic Chianti Classico or Brunello di Montalcino with typical Tuscan foods like Bistecca alla Fiorentina (Florentine steak), Pappa al Pomodoro (tomato and bread soup), or Pecorino cheese.

- **Piedmont**: Match the strong flavors of Barolo or Barbaresco with Piedmontese meals like Brasato al Barolo (beef cooked in Barolo wine), Tajarin pasta with truffle sauce, or aged Parmigiano-Reggiano.

- **Veneto**: Accompany Venetian delicacies such as Risotto al Nero di Seppia (squid ink risotto) or Baccalà Mantecato (creamed salted fish) with a refreshing glass of Soave or Valpolicella.
- **Sicily**: Pair the robust and fruity Nero d'Avola with Sicilian delicacies like linguine alla Norma (linguine with eggplant and ricotta salata), Caponata (sweet and sour eggplant relish), or cannoli.

5. **Experimenting and Personal Preferences**: While the broad rules and geographical pairings give a starting point, wine, and food matching are also about personal taste and experimentation. Don't be scared to test various combinations and discover what works best for you. Attend wine tastings, tour local vineyards, and speak with sommeliers or local experts to increase your expertise and find hidden treasures.

Remember, the most essential component of wine and food matching is to enjoy the experience and create harmonious pairings that improve both the tastes of the food and the wine. Italy's rich culinary traditions and various wine choices give limitless options for research and pleasure.

- Dining Etiquette and Tips

Dining in Italy is not only about excellent cuisine; it's also a cultural experience that bears its own set of etiquette and traditions. Italians take their meals seriously and see eating as a time for leisure, mingling, and enjoying the tastes. To help you make the most of your dining experience in Italy, here is a detailed reference on dining etiquette and tips:

1. **Making Reservations**: In popular restaurants, it's important to make reservations in advance, particularly during peak hours and tourist seasons. Italians value punctuality, so come on time or a few minutes early to fulfill your reservation.

2. **Dressing Appropriately**: Italians often dress beautifully for supper, particularly at luxury establishments. While casual gear is allowed in certain locations, it's always a good idea to dress smartly and avoid extremely casual or beachwear apparel.

3. **Greetings and Seating**: When entering a restaurant, it's nice to greet the employees with a cordial "Buongiorno" (good morning) or "Buona sera" (good evening). Wait to be seated by the host or maître d', and don't sit at a table until you're told to do so.

4. **Table Manners**: - Bread and Olive Oil: In Italian restaurants, bread is often provided without butter. Instead, dip it in the olive oil given on the table, but avoid stocking up on bread before the meal.

- **Utensil Usage**: Italians use both a fork and a knife when eating, with the fork held in the left hand and the knife in the right. Switching the fork to the right hand after cutting food is considered disrespectful.

- **Spaghetti and Long Pasta**: Use a fork to spin the pasta onto your spoon. Avoid cutting lengthy spaghetti with a knife, and never suck it straight off the dish.

- **Pizza**: When eating pizza, it's normal to eat it with your hands, not with a knife and fork.

- **Cheese with Seafood**: Avoid adding cheese to seafood meals, since it is often considered a faux pas in Italy.

5. **Pace of the Meal**: Italians like unhurried dinners and believe in savoring each dish. Don't

hurry through your lunch; take your time to savor the food, participate in the conversation, and embrace the easygoing ambiance.

6. **Wine and Water**: - Ordering Wine: In Italy, wine is a vital element of the dining experience. Feel free to ask the waiter for wine suggestions depending on your meal selections. If you prefer water, you may order "acqua naturale" (still water) or "acqua frizzante" (sparkling water).

- **Toasting**: When toasting, establish eye contact with each individual at the table and say "cin cin" or "salute." It's usual to clink glasses with everyone individually rather than across the table.

7. **Tipping**: Service costs are frequently included in the bill in Italy. However, it's normal to leave a little tip as a sign of gratitude for great service. This is normally roughly 5-10% of the entire price. Leave the tip in cash immediately on the table or inform the waiter of the whole amount you intend to pay, including the tip.

8. **Engaging with the Staff**: Italians respect personal relationships and like amicable encounters. Engage with the personnel nicely

and respectfully, use simple Italian words like "Grazie" (thank you), "per favor" (please), and "scuba" (excuse me), and express your gratitude for the service.

9. **Enjoying the Digestive**: After dinner, it's typical to indulge in a digestive, such as limoncello or amaro, to ease digestion. These are frequently offered as a nice gift from the eatery.

10. **Splitting the cost**: In Italy, it's not typical to divide the cost separately. Instead, the cost is frequently shared evenly among all diners, unless particular agreements have been made in advance.

Remember, eating in Italy is a social occasion designed to be savored and enjoyed. By following the local traditions and enjoying the unhurried pace of the dinner, you'll not only have a great gastronomic experience but also develop a better knowledge of Italian culture.

- Cooking Classes and Food Tours

Italy is known for its rich culinary tradition and is frequently considered a paradise for food lovers. From classic pasta meals to artisan cheeses, fragrant wines, and gelato, Italian food has captured the hearts and taste buds of people worldwide. To truly immerse oneself in the culinary pleasures of Italy, there's no better approach than to enroll in cooking workshops and food excursions. In this post, we will examine the wonderful chances available for food fans to participate in genuine experiences and understand the secrets of Italian cuisine.

1. **Food lessons in Italy**:

1.1. **Diversity of Culinary Experiences**: Italy provides a broad selection of culinary lessons that appeal to diverse tastes and interests. Whether you're interested in studying the art of pizza-making in Naples, honing the skills of fresh pasta in Tuscany, or investigating the secrets of regional delicacies, there is a cooking class for everyone.

1.2. **Expert Instruction from Local Chefs**: These sessions are often given by experienced local chefs who are enthusiastic about sharing their expertise and culinary traditions. They give hands-on coaching, teaching you the methods, ingredients, and cultural importance behind each recipe. You'll get the chance to cook classic dishes from scratch and develop a greater appreciation of Italian culinary history.

1.3. Market Visits and Ingredient Sourcing: Many cooking workshops include a visit to local markets, where you may observe the brilliant colors and fragrances of fresh vegetables, fish, meats, and spices. You'll learn how to pick the best ingredients and acquire insights into the significance of quality sourcing in Italian cuisine.

1.4. Regional specialties and diversified Menus: Italy's food is very diversified, with each area claiming its distinct tastes and specialties. Cooking workshops enable you to explore these regional differences and produce recipes that represent the culinary traditions of certain locations. Whether it's risotto in Lombardy, pesto in Liguria, or cannoli in Sicily, you'll discover the different tastes that make Italian food so special.

2. Food Tours in Italy:

2.1. Guided Gastronomic Adventures: Food tours provide a full overview of Italy's gastronomic environment, bringing you beyond conventional tourist locations. Led by skilled interpreters, these trips dig into local cuisine culture, history, and customs. You'll see hidden jewels, family-owned cafés, and handmade businesses that are typically ignored by travelers.

2.2. **Regional and Cultural Discoveries**: Italy's numerous regions each have their distinct culinary character. Food tours give a chance to sample these regional delicacies firsthand. Whether it's indulging in the substantial cuisine of Emilia-Romagna, eating street food in Rome, or experiencing the seafood pleasures of the Amalfi Coast, you'll get a better appreciation for the various tastes that distinguish each area.

2.3. **Wine and Cheese Tastings**: No gastronomic vacation in Italy is complete without sampling the country's renowned wines and cheeses. Food tours sometimes include excursions to wineries and cheese factories, where you may learn about the manufacturing processes and enjoy the tastes of local types. From Chianti in Tuscany to Barolo in Piedmont, and Parmigiano-Reggiano in Emilia-Romagna, you'll find the precise matches that enhance Italian food.

2.4. **Cultural Immersion**: Food is tightly woven into the fabric of Italian culture. Food tours give chances to connect with people, building a greater knowledge of their customs and way of life. Whether it's joining a family for a traditional dinner, participating in olive oil or wine festivals, or studying the origins of classic dishes, you'll immerse yourself in the rich cultural fabric that surrounds Italian food.

In conclusion, Going on a cooking class or culinary tour in Italy is a great opportunity to increase your understanding of Italian cuisine. Through hands-on experiences, professional instruction, and investigation of regional specialties, you'll get a comprehensive grasp of the tastes, methods, and cultural importance that make Italian cuisine so adored globally. From pasta-making in Tuscany to enjoying gelato in Florence or experiencing the bustling marketplaces of Naples, the culinary delights that await in Italy are guaranteed to make an everlasting imprint on your palette and heart.

CHAPTER 6. Discovering Italian Culture

- Italian Art and Architecture

Italy is famous internationally for its rich and important contributions to the realms of art and architecture. From ancient Roman monuments to Renaissance masterpieces, Italy's creative and architectural legacy spans centuries and continues to inspire and enchant audiences today. This comprehensive material will present an introduction to Italian art and architecture, covering significant eras, artists, and notable masterpieces.

1. **Ancient Roman Art and Architecture**: Italy's creative history extends back to ancient times, with the Romans, left a lasting imprint on art and architecture. Roman architecture is typified by magnificent constructions such as the Colosseum, the Pantheon, and the aqueducts. These constructions showed great technical achievements and demonstrated the Romans' mastery of arches, vaults, and domes. Roman art, including sculpture and mosaics, typically featured historical events, mythical beings, and emperors.

2. **Byzantine and Early Christian Art**: During the Byzantine period, Italy gained artistic influences from the eastern Mediterranean. This time witnessed the creation of exquisite mosaics in churches, such as the Basilica of San Vitale in Ravenna, famed for its bright Byzantine mosaics portraying religious themes and characters. Early Christian art in Italy integrated biblical storytelling and symbolism, frequently visible in frescoes and illuminated manuscripts.

3. **Gothic Art and Architecture**: The Gothic era in Italy, spanning the 13th to 15th centuries, offered a new style defined by pointed arches, ribbed vaults, and flying buttresses. Notable examples of Italian Gothic architecture are the Milan Cathedral and the Florence Cathedral, both possessing complex façades and towering spires. In art, the Gothic style is represented in church murals and sculptures, with painters like Cimabue and Giotto leading the way.

4. **Renaissance Art and Architecture**: The Italian Renaissance, regarded as one of the most important eras in art history, originated in the 14th century and thrived during the 15th and 16th centuries. The Renaissance was distinguished by a revitalized interest in ancient antiquities, humanism, and scientific

investigation, leading to remarkable developments in art and architecture.

a. **Renaissance Architecture**: Prominent architects like Filippo Brunelleschi and Leon Battista Alberti devised ideas of perspective, proportion, and harmony, changing the architectural design. Examples of Renaissance architecture include Florence's Palazzo Medici Riccardi and the Palazzo Farnese in Rome. The time also saw the creation of prominent structures such as St. Peter's Basilica in Vatican City, constructed by Michelangelo and other renowned architects.

b. **Renaissance Art**: Italy's Renaissance produced some of the world's finest artists, including Leonardo da Vinci, Michelangelo, and Raphael. Leonardo's "Mona Lisa" and "The Last Supper," Michelangelo's Sistine Chapel ceiling, and Raphael's murals in the Vatican's Raphael Rooms are masterpieces that epitomize the period. Artists of the period concentrated on realism, perspective, and human anatomy, producing realistic paintings and sculptures that represented the essence of the human form.

5. **Baroque Art and Architecture**: The Baroque era, developing in the late 16th century, gave a more dynamic and dramatic

style to Italian art and architecture. Baroque architecture is distinguished by extravagant decorations, dramatic lighting, and the imaginative use of space. The masterpieces of Gian Lorenzo Bernini, such as St. Peter's Square in Vatican City and the Ecstasy of Saint Teresa in Rome, embody the grandeur and emotional intensity of the Baroque style. Baroque art generally emphasized religious themes and utilized great contrasts of light and shadow to create a feeling of drama.

6. **Neoclassical and Romantic Art**: The 18th and 19th centuries in Italy saw a Renaissance of interest in ancient antiquity, leading to the Neoclassical movement. Architects like Andrea Palladio and Antonio Canova adopted classical forms and proportions, inspiring structures such as the Teatro alla Scala in Milan and the Tempio Canoviano in Possagno. Romantic painters, like Francesco Hayez, emphasized emotional expressiveness and historical topics, expressing the romantic ideals of the period.

7. **Modern and Contemporary Art and Architecture**: In the 20th century, Italy continued to contribute to the art and architectural scene. Architects like Gio Ponti and Renzo Piano developed unique ideas,

blending usefulness and beauty. Noteworthy modern constructions include the Pompidou Center in Paris, built by Renzo Piano, and the MAXXI National Museum of XXI Century Arts in Rome, created by Zaha Hadid.

Italian painters like Amedeo Modigliani, Giorgio de Chirico, and Lucio Fontana made major contributions to modern and contemporary art movements. Italy also features world-renowned art institutions such as the Uffizi Gallery in Florence and the Peggy Guggenheim Collection in Venice, which holds enormous collections of Italian and foreign artworks.

In conclusion, Italian art and architecture have left an everlasting influence on the history of aesthetic expression. From the ancient Romans to the Renaissance masters and beyond, Italy's cultural accomplishments continue to fascinate and inspire audiences worldwide. The country's rich and diversified creative past remains a significant element of worldwide cultural heritage.

- Opera and Music

Italy has a deep and storied past when it comes to opera and music. The nation is largely considered the home of opera, and its impact on the art form is unsurpassed. Italian composers, performers, and opera houses have made enormous contributions to the creation and evolution of opera, establishing Italy as a magnet for operatic fans globally. In addition to opera, Italy has also produced some of the world's most famous classical composers and artists.

Opera in Italy: Opera, a dramatic art form combining music and theater, emerged in Italy in the late 16th century during the Renaissance. It swiftly acquired popularity and became a vital component of Italian culture. The first opera, "Dafne" by Jacopo Peri, was performed in Florence in 1598. However, it was Claudio Monteverdi's masterpieces, notably "L'Orfeo" (1607) and "Il ritorno d'Ulisse in patria" (1640), that marked the birth of opera as we know it today.

Italian opera is noted for its melodic richness, emotional depth, and expressive singing. The Bel canto ("beautiful singing") style, created in the early 19th century, stressed virtuoso vocal performances, lyrical melodies, and vocal elaboration. This style reached its apex with composers like Gioachino Rossini, Vincenzo Bellini, and Gaetano Donizetti, whose works are still performed frequently in opera houses across the globe.

Italian Opera Houses: Italy is home to various old and prominent opera houses, some of which have become iconic emblems of the art form. One of the most famous is La Scala in Milan, which opened in 1778 and has featured world-renowned artists and debuts of many notable operas. Other noteworthy opera theaters include Teatro San Carlo in Naples, Teatro dell'Opera di Roma, Teatro Regio in Turin, and Teatro La Fenice in Venice. These venues present both traditional repertoire and modern performances, drawing opera aficionados from all around the world.

Famous Italian Composers: Italy has produced an astonishing number of famous composers whose compositions continue to enchant listeners. Here are a handful of the most notable:

1. **Giuseppe Verdi (1813-1901):** Verdi is regarded as one of the finest opera composers of all time. His masterpieces, like "La Traviata,"

"Rigoletto," and "Aida," are classics of the opera repertory.

2. **Giacomo Puccini (1858-1924)**: Puccini's operas, notably "La Bohème," "Tosca," and "Madama Butterfly," are recognized for their sumptuous orchestrations and heartbreaking narrative.

3. **Wolfgang Amadeus Mozart (1756-1791)**: Although not Italian himself, Mozart spent substantial time in Italy and created numerous notable operas, such as "The Marriage of Figaro" and "Don Giovanni," which helped define the Italian opera tradition.

4. **Gioachino Rossini (1792-1868)**: Rossini's comedic operas, such as "The Barber of Seville" and "La Cenerentola," are known for their vibrant and lyrical melodies.

5. **Vincenzo Bellini (1801-1835)**: Bellini's operas, notably "Norma" and "I Puritani," are appreciated for their lovely melodies and emotional depth.

Contemporary Italian Music: Italy's musical tradition goes beyond opera. The nation has also produced significant composers and artists in different genres, including classical, current, and popular music. Luciano Berio, Luigi Nono, and Salvatore Sciarrino are notable Italian composers who have created major contributions to current classical music. Additionally, Italian popular music has achieved success both locally and abroad, with musicians such as Eros Ramazzotti, Laura Pausini, and Andrea Bocelli gaining worldwide acclaim.

Music Festivals in Italy: Italy has various music festivals throughout the year, drawing music fans from across the globe. The Arena di Verona Opera Festival, hosted in Verona's historic Roman amphitheater, is one of the most renowned opera events, showcasing spectacular performances in a stunning setting. The Ravenna Festival features a varied spectrum of music, including classical, jazz, and world music. Other famous events include the Puccini Festival in Torre del Lago, Umbria Jazz Festival in Perugia, and the Rossini Opera Festival in Pesaro.

In conclusion, Opera and music are profoundly interwoven in the cultural fabric of Italy. The country's contributions to opera, from its roots through the Bel canto period and beyond, have left an unmistakable influence on the art form. Italy's great opera theaters continue to offer outstanding performances, while its composers and artists have molded the landscape of classical and modern music. Whether studying the masterpieces of Verdi and Puccini or visiting a dynamic music festival, Italy provides a riveting experience for opera and music aficionados alike.

- Festivals and Celebrations

Italy is a nation noted for its rich cultural history and lively customs. Festivals and festivities play a vital part in Italian culture, looking into the country's history, traditions, and regional variety. From religious processions to colorful carnivals, Italy organizes a broad variety of events throughout the year. Here, we shall examine some of the most prominent festivals and events in Italy.

1. **Carnival of Venice**: Held in Venice, this world-renowned carnival takes place in the weeks leading up to Lent. Participants assume elaborate masks and costumes, bringing an aura of mystery and intrigue to the city's canals and squares. Visitors may enjoy street entertainment, music, and local cuisine, and see the famed masquerade parade.

2. **Easter Celebrations**: Easter retains tremendous importance in Italy, and local towns have distinct rituals to honor the holiday. In Florence, the Scoppio del Carro (Explosion of the Cart) comprises a magnificent parade preceding a wagon laden with fireworks that are fired to guarantee a prosperous crop. In Rome, the Pope leads the Easter Sunday Mass in St. Peter's Square, attracting throngs of people from across the globe.

3. **Infiorata events**: Infiorata, meaning "flowered," is a series of events that take place throughout Italy during the summer months. Streets are covered with exquisite flower carpets, generating lovely motifs and patterns. The most renowned Infiorata festivities are in Spello, Genzano, and Noto, where artisans methodically arrange petals to create breathtaking artwork.

4. **Feast of Saint John**: Celebrated on June 24th, the Feast of Saint John (Festa di San Giovanni) is a traditional celebration that began in Florence but is commemorated in other locations of Italy. Festivities generally include parades, fireworks, bonfires, and the famed Calcio Storico (historical football) competition,

a traditional game that mixes aspects of soccer, rugby, and wrestling.

5. **Palio di Siena**: Held in the historic city of Siena, Tuscany, the Palio is a spectacular horse race that takes place twice a year, on July 2nd and August 16th. The race is a tough fight between the city's 17 districts, known as contrade, each represented by a jockey riding bareback. The Palio draws hundreds of fans who congregate in Siena's ancient Piazza del Campo to cheer for their preferred Contrada.

6. **La Notte Rosa**: Translated as "The Pink Night," this event takes place along the Adriatic coast in Emilia-Romagna and Marche districts. Held on the first weekend of July, the festival celebrates summer and incorporates music, fireworks, street entertainment, and art displays. The whole coastline comes alive with a festive atmosphere, and tourists may enjoy the loud beach parties and bright decorations.

7. **Festa della Madonna Bruna**: Celebrated in the southern city of Matera, Basilicata, this event commemorates the city's patron saint, the Madonna Bruna. On July 2nd, a procession of hundreds of people takes a large figure of the Madonna through the streets of Matera, ending in a spectacular conclusion when the monument

is set on fire. The event is a unique combination of religious devotion and spectacle.

8. **Feast of the Assumption**: Celebrated on August 15th, the Feast of the Assumption (Ferragosto) honors the Catholic belief in the Virgin Mary's ascent into heaven. This national public holiday is extensively recognized in Italy, with many people taking vacations and enjoying outdoor sports. Firework displays, beach parties, and cultural activities are widespread across the nation.

9. **Grape Harvest Celebrations**: Italy's wine-producing areas celebrate the grape harvest with lively celebrations known as " Festival delle uve." These events, conducted from late August to early October, provide visitors the chance to participate in grape harvesting, traditional wine pressing, and tasting sessions. Notable grape harvest festivities may be found in Piedmont, Tuscany, and Sicily.

10. **Christmas Marketplaces**: During the Christmas season, towns throughout Italy come alive with festive marketplaces, known as "mercatini di Natale." These markets contain vendors offering crafts, decorations, and traditional cuisine specialties. The most

renowned Christmas markets are situated in Trento, Bolzano, and Bologna, allowing tourists a chance to enjoy the magical ambiance of the holiday season.

These are just a few instances of the various festivals and festivities that take place throughout Italy. Whether it's a historical tradition, a religious event, or a cultural celebration, each festival gives a unique glimpse into the country's distinct traditions and past. Visitors visiting Italy may immerse themselves in the vivid atmosphere of these festivals, generating unique experiences and acquiring a greater understanding of the country's rich cultural tapestry.

- Fashion and Shopping

Italy is famous globally for its fashion sector, and its cities are regarded as global fashion capitals. From luxurious luxury brands to quirky shops, Italy provides a broad and exciting shopping experience for fashion fans. Whether you're visiting Rome, Milan, Florence, or other Italian towns, you'll discover a wealth of alternatives to explore and indulge in the current fashion trends. Here is a thorough reference on fashion and shopping in Italy.

1. **Italian Fashion businesses**: Italy is home to some of the most renowned and influential fashion businesses in the world. Names like Gucci, Prada, Armani, Versace, Dolce & Gabbana, Valentino, and Fendi have become associated with luxury and flair. These businesses present their newest collections at their flagship shops, giving an immersive experience for fashion fans.

2. **Luxury retail Districts**: Italy's largest cities feature luxury retail districts that draw customers from all over the world. In Milan, the Quadrilatero della Moda (Fashion Quadrilateral) is a must-visit, containing iconic avenues like Via Montenapoleone, Via della Spiga, Via Manzoni, and Corso Venezia. In Rome, Via Condotti near the Spanish Steps is famed for its high-end stores, including designer names like Bulgari and Fendi. Florence's Via de' Tornabuoni is another prominent retail route, boasting brands like Gucci, Salvatore Ferragamo, and Roberto Cavalli.

3. **Concept shops**: Italy is recognized for its inventive and cutting-edge concept shops that provide a handpicked variety of fashion, design, and lifestyle items. One example is 10 Corso Como in Milan, a multi-functional venue integrating retail, gallery, café, and bookstore. Excelsior Milano is another prominent concept store in Milan, giving a unique shopping experience spanning seven stories, combining fashion, beauty, design, and gastronomy.

4. **Outlet Shopping**: If you're seeking designer discounts, Italy boasts various outlet shopping sites. The most renowned is the Serravalle Designer Outlet, situated between Milan and Genoa. This outlet town features over 300 worldwide brands, giving savings on past seasons' selections. Other prominent outlets include The Mall near Florence, where you can discover premium goods like Prada and Gucci, and Barberino Designer Outlet, also near Florence.

5. **Local Markets**: Italy's local markets are a treasure mine of unique fashion treasures. Mercato di Porta Portese in Rome is one of Europe's biggest flea markets, offering vintage clothes, accessories, and antiques. Florence's San Lorenzo Market is known for leather items,

including purses, coats, and shoes. In Venice, the Mercerie alleys around St. Mark's Square provide a range of stores offering Venetian masks, Murano glass, and lace items.

6. **Made in Italy**: Italy is known for its craftsmanship and excellence in fashion creation. When buying in Italy, check for the "Made in Italy" mark, which certifies the authenticity and exceptional workmanship of the goods. From gorgeous leather goods and shoes to luxury linens and accessories, choosing locally-made items assures you're investing in the greatest Italian workmanship.

7. **Fashion Events**: Italy holds many fashion events throughout the year, bringing industry experts and fashion fans from across the globe. Milan Fashion Week and Pitti Immagine Uomo in Florence are two noteworthy events exhibiting the newest collections from established designers and upcoming talents. These events look at future trends and enable fashion fans to immerse themselves in the bustling Italian fashion industry.

8. **Personal Shopping and Styling**: Many fashion-conscious travelers to Italy take advantage of personal shopping and styling services given by specialists. Personal shoppers

may aid you in choosing the appropriate clothing and accessories according to your style and preferences. They frequently have deep knowledge of local fashion hotspots and can take you through the fashion panorama of Italy.

In conclusion, fashion and shopping in Italy provide a varied and diversified experience. Whether you're searching for high-end luxury goods, unusual shops, or local market treasures, Italy offers something for everyone. Immerse yourself in the world of Italian fashion, visit the luxury shopping districts, discover concept shops, and experience the attraction of "Made in Italy" workmanship. Enjoy the exciting fashion events and engage in customized shopping experiences, creating memories and a wardrobe inspired by the classic elegance of Italy.

- Sports and Recreation

Italy is a nation recognized for its rich history, gorgeous scenery, and lively culture. When it comes to sports and amusement, Italy provides a vast assortment of activities that appeal to both residents and visitors alike. From football to racing, from skiing to water sports, Italy offers countless chances for citizens to participate in physical activities and enjoy the wonderful outdoors. Whether you are a sports fanatic or just seeking to have some fun, Italy has something to offer everyone.

1. **Football (Calcio)**: Football, or calcio as it is called in Italy, is the most popular sport in the nation. Italians are enthusiastic about football, and the nation enjoys a robust sport with a long heritage. Italy has produced some of the world's best football players, and the national team has enjoyed incredible success, winning the FIFA World Cup four times. Serie A, the top-tier professional football competition in Italy, draws millions of spectators from across the globe. Attending a football match in Italy is an amazing experience, with passionate crowds, strong rivalries, and outstanding venues.

2. **Racing**: Italy has a big presence in the world of racing, with Formula 1 and MotoGP being the most popular categories. The renowned Monza Circuit in Milan holds the Italian Grand Prix, attracting racing lovers from throughout the world. Italian racing teams, such as Ferrari and Ducati, have achieved considerable success and have a passionate fan following. Additionally, there are several karting circuits and racing events hosted around the nation,

enabling anyone to experience the excitement of driving on the track.

3. **Cycling**: Italy's stunning landscapes and tough terrains make it a perfect destination for cycling aficionados. The nation is host to major cycling events like the Giro d'Italia, one of the three Grand Tours in professional cycling. From stunning seaside routes to alpine passes, Italy offers different cycling routes ideal for all levels of cyclists. Cycling excursions and rental services are offered, enabling tourists to explore the countryside and appreciate the beauty of Italy at their leisure.

4. **Skiing and Winter Sports**: Italy is known for its gorgeous ski resorts set in the breathtaking Italian Alps. The Dolomites, situated in northeastern Italy, provide world-class skiing and snowboarding options. Popular ski resorts include Cortina d'Ampezzo, Val Gardena, and Madonna di Campiglio. Ski resorts in Italy feature well-groomed slopes, contemporary amenities, and stunning mountain views. Apart from skiing, guests may also indulge in sports such as ice skating, snowshoeing, and cross-country skiing.

5. **Water Sports**: With a lengthy coastline along the Mediterranean Sea, Italy provides a variety of water sports activities. Sailing, windsurfing, and kitesurfing are popular along the shores of places such as Sardinia, Sicily, and Liguria. The crystal-clear waters offer great conditions for scuba diving and snorkeling, enabling people to discover rich marine life and underwater caverns. Coastal communities also provide chances for fishing, kayaking, and paddleboarding.

6. **Basketball, Volleyball, and Rugby**: While football takes center stage, Italy also has a significant presence in other team sports. Basketball, volleyball, and rugby are popular and have a passionate fan following. The Italian basketball league, Lega Basket Serie A, shows top-level skill and draws fervent spectators. Volleyball is extensively played at both amateur and professional levels, with Italy routinely competing among the best in international championships. Rugby has gained popularity in recent years, and the Italian national team participates in the Six Nations Championship.

7. **Tennis and Golf**: Italy features various tennis and golf clubs, giving opportunities for both leisure and competitive players. The Italian

Open, part of the ATP World Tour Masters 1000 series, is a notable tennis event recruiting top-ranked players. Golf aficionados may enjoy lush courses set against gorgeous backgrounds, with Tuscany and Lake Como being especially popular destinations for playing.

8. **Traditional Sports and Games**: Italy has a rich legacy of traditional sports and games that represent its cultural past. One such example is bocce, a famous Italian ball sport comparable to lawn bowling. Bocce courts may be found in numerous parks and small villages around the nation. Calcio Storico, a medieval version of football going back to the 16th century, is another ancient sport specific to Italy. It mixes aspects of football, rugby, and wrestling and is played yearly in Florence.

In conclusion, Italy provides a varied choice of sports and leisure activities that appeal to all interests and ability levels. Whether you like watching or playing, the country's enthusiasm for sports is obvious in its athletic events, facilities, and ardent spectators. From the thrill of football matches to the tranquility of cycling through stunning landscapes, Italy gives various chances for people to engage in their favorite activities and enjoy the delight of leisure.

CHAPTER 7. Outdoor Adventures in Italy

- Hiking in the Dolomites

The Dolomites, a spectacular mountain range located in northeastern Italy, are famous worldwide for their stunning beauty and awe-inspiring sceneries. Hiking in the Dolomites provides an amazing outdoor experience, where towering peaks, cliffs, green valleys, and beautiful alpine lakes meet to create a hiker's dream. Whether you're an expert climber or a nature enthusiast seeking peace, the Dolomites provide a vast selection of hiking paths to suit every skill level and desire. In this thorough book, we will explore the gorgeous Dolomites area, dig into its distinctive qualities, highlight some of the most popular hiking routes, and give practical advice to help you plan and make the most of your hiking journey.

The Dolomites: A UNESCO World Heritage Site: Designated as a UNESCO World Past Site in 2009, the Dolomites attract tourists with their remarkable natural beauty, geological importance, and rich cultural past. Comprising numerous separate mountain ranges, including the Sella, Marmolada, and Tre Cime di Lavaredo, the Dolomites highlight a particular rock formation known as dolomite, which gives the mountains their unique look. These towering peaks, frequently bathed in shades of pink and orange at dawn and sunset, offer an exquisite background for hikers as they explore the region's routes.

Hiking paths for All Levels: The Dolomites feature an extensive network of well-marked hiking paths that cater to all ability levels, ranging from pleasant strolls through alpine meadows to demanding ascents of steep peaks. Here are some of the popular hiking paths in the Dolomites:

1. **Tre Cime di Lavaredo Circuit**: One of the most recognizable routes in the Dolomites, this circular track takes you around the beautiful Tre Cime di Lavaredo, a trio of unique peaks. The walk provides stunning views of jagged rock formations, glacial valleys, and crystal-clear lakes.

2. **Alta Via 1**: For experienced hikers wanting a multi-day adventure, the Alta Via 1 is an epic walk lasting around 150 kilometers. It spans the heart of the Dolomites, passing steep mountain

passes, green valleys, and lovely alpine communities.

3. **Seceda Ridgeline**: This moderate climb takes you along the magnificent Seceda ridgeline, affording panoramic views of the surrounding hills and valleys. The route is especially famed for its breathtaking sights during the fall season when the foliage turns into vivid colors of red and gold.

4. **Lake Braies Circuit:** Located near the picturesque Lake Braies, this easy circular walk offers hikers to explore the quiet beaches of the lake, surrounded by lush woods and high mountains. The blue waters of Lake Braies provide a beautiful reflection of the surrounding Alps.

5. **Tre Cime Nature Park**: Situated in the Sexten Dolomites, this nature park provides a choice of routes ideal for various fitness levels. From easy treks to strenuous climbs, hikers may explore spectacular alpine scenery, and alpine flora, and possibly glimpse some species along the route.

Note: It's crucial to analyze your fitness level, experience, and the complexity of each path before beginning on a trek. Weather conditions and seasons may dramatically alter trail accessibility, therefore it's essential to verify local circumstances and contact local authorities or expert guides before heading out.

Practical Considerations:

1. **Best Time to Hike**: The Dolomites are best explored from late spring to early fall (May to October), when the weather is typically good and the routes are accessible. However, the summer months (July and August) tend to be the busiest, so try trekking during the shoulder seasons (May-June, and September-October) for a calmer experience.

2. **Housing**: The Dolomites provide several housing alternatives, including mountain huts (rifugi), hotels, and guesthouses. It's important to reserve your lodgings in advance, particularly during high seasons, to assure availability.

3. **Safety Precautions**: Hiking in the mountains demands appropriate preparation and preventative measures. Carry necessary items such as proper clothes, strong hiking boots, a map, a compass, and lots of water and snacks. Be careful of weather changes, heed route markers, and respect the environment and animals.

4. **Local Culture and Cuisine**: The Dolomites are home to a thriving local culture and provide

a gourmet feast for food connoisseurs. Embrace the chance to sample traditional delicacies like polenta, speck (cured ham), and substantial mountain cuisine offered at the rifugi. Respect local traditions and be sensitive to the environment, following the ideals of "Leave No Trace" to preserve the beauty of the Dolomites for future generations.

In conclusion, hiking in the Dolomites is a genuinely immersive and compelling experience that enables you to connect with nature, push yourself physically, and absorb the majesty of one of the world's most amazing mountain ranges. From leisurely hikes through alpine meadows to exhilarating ascents of towering peaks, the Dolomites provide an experience for every sort of hiker. So, lace on boots, bring out the cool alpine air and begin trekking adventure across the stunning landscapes of the Dolomites.

- Cycling in Tuscany

Tuscany, a region in central Italy, is famed for its gorgeous scenery, scenic countryside, lovely ancient towns, and exquisite food. It is also a terrific location for bicycle aficionados. With its rolling hills, vineyards, olive orchards, and old towns, Tuscany provides a unique and enjoyable riding experience. Whether you're a casual cyclist or a committed rider, there are routes and itineraries to suit all levels of expertise and fitness.

Cycling Routes:

1. **Chianti Loop**: The Chianti area, famed for its wine production, provides some of the most attractive cycling routes in Tuscany. The circle begins and finishes in the picturesque city of Florence, bringing you vineyards, cypress-lined lanes, and ancient hilltop villages such as Greve and Castellina in Chianti. Along the journey, you may stop at wineries for tastings and enjoy panoramic views of the Tuscan countryside.

2. **Val d'Orcia**: Located in the southern portion of Tuscany, the Val d'Orcia is a UNESCO World Heritage site famed for its rolling hills, quaint towns, and famous cypress trees. The trip takes you past cities like Montalcino, Pienza, and Montepulciano, affording spectacular views of the environment. This region is also famed for its Brunello di Montalcino wine, which you may enjoy at nearby wineries.

3. **Lucca to Pisa**: This route unites two classic Tuscan towns and is generally flat, making it

suited for cyclists of all abilities. Starting in Lucca, a picturesque walled city with small streets and gorgeous squares, you'll bike through the countryside, through vineyards and olive trees. The tour concludes at Pisa, where you may view the iconic Leaning Tower and other architectural wonders.

4. **Florence to Siena**: This tough route brings you into the heart of Tuscany, linking two of its most attractive towns. Starting in Florence, you'll ride through the rolling hills of the Chianti area before reaching Siena, a historic city noted for its Palio horse race and spectacular Gothic architecture. The journey provides stunning views and an opportunity to see tiny Tuscan towns along the way.

5. **Coastline Ride**: If you prefer a coastline ride, Tuscany provides stunning routes along the Tyrrhenian Sea. Starting in Livorno, you may bike down the coast, passing through picturesque coastal villages like Castiglioncello, Cecina, and San Vincenzo. You'll have the chance to enjoy spectacular views of the sea, stop for a dip, and indulge in fresh seafood at local eateries.

Cycling Services and Infrastructure:

Tuscany caters to bikers with its well-developed infrastructure and services. You'll find several bike rental businesses in major cities and towns, providing a choice of bikes ideal for varied terrains and tastes. It's best to book your bike in advance, particularly during high tourist seasons.

The area also includes a vast network of bike trails and approved routes, making it safer and more pleasurable for cyclists. Many of these routes are well-marked and include a blend of paved roads and gravel trails, enabling cyclists to pick their chosen degree of effort.

Tuscany is host to various cycling competitions and tours throughout the year. The Eroica, a classic cycling race conducted yearly in Gaiole in Chianti, draws riders from across the globe. It honors the spirit of cycling with participants riding antique bikes around the beautiful white gravel roads of the area.

Tips for Cycling in Tuscany:

1. **Safety**: Always wear a helmet, respect traffic regulations, and be careful when sharing the road with other vehicles. Use reflective clothing and lights while riding during low-light situations.

2. **Bike Maintenance**: Ensure your bike is in excellent condition before going out on your riding excursion. Carry a puncture repair kit, extra tubes, and essential equipment for simple repairs.

3. **Hydration and Nutrition**: Stay hydrated and bring adequate water and food, particularly during long rides in the Tuscan heat. Take pauses at local cafés or trattorias to enjoy regional delicacies and recharge your energies.

4. **Season and Weather**: Tuscany has pleasant winters and scorching summers. Plan your bicycle vacation appropriately, taking into consideration the weather conditions and the ideal time to visit. Spring (April to June) and fall (September to October) are popular seasons for cycling in Tuscany owing to cooler weather and fewer people.

5. **Explore the Local Culture**: Take the opportunity to immerse yourself in the Tuscan culture and explore the picturesque villages along your bike path. Explore local markets, sample traditional Tuscan food, and visit historic landmarks to improve your whole experience.

Cycling in Tuscany provides a unique chance to experience the region's natural beauty, uncover its rich history, and enjoy its gastronomic pleasures. Whether you pick a relaxing ride through the vineyards or a tough route through the hills, Tuscany delivers amazing cycling excursions for cyclists of all abilities. So take your bike, bask in the gorgeous views, and let Tuscany's charm enchant you as you cycle around this lovely area of Italy.

- Water Sports along the Coast

Italy, with its gorgeous coastline along the Mediterranean Sea, provides a variety of choices for water sports fans. Whether you are an adrenaline junkie or seeking a more calm aquatic experience, Italy's coastal areas give a range of possibilities to suit your tastes. From the unambiguous seas of Sardinia to the scenic Amalfi Coast, these are some of the popular water sports activities you can enjoy along the coast of Italy.

1. **Snorkeling and Scuba Diving**: Italy's coastal waters are noted for their rich marine biodiversity and thriving undersea habitats. Snorkeling and scuba diving enables you to discover the hidden gems under the sea's surface. The island of Sardinia, notably the

Costa Smeralda and La Maddalena Archipelago, provides some of the greatest diving places in Italy. The Amalfi Coast and the Aeolian Islands also present fantastic possibilities to find unique aquatic life, old shipwrecks, and breathtaking underwater caverns.

2. **Sailing & Yachting**: With its rich history of nautical heritage, Italy is a haven for sailing aficionados. The Amalfi Coast, with its spectacular cliffs and colorful cities, offers a stunning setting for a sailing trip. The Italian Riviera, including Portofino and Cinque Terre, provides stunning ports and spectacular vistas. Sardinia's Costa Smeralda is famous for its luxury yachting culture, drawing sailing fans from across the globe. Additionally, the lovely islands of Sicily and Capri are also popular locations for sailing holidays.

3. **Windsurfing and Kitesurfing**: The coastal areas of Italy are well-known for their steady winds, making them excellent for windsurfing and kitesurfing. Lake Garda, situated in northern Italy, is one of the most recognized windsurfing sites in Europe. The high winds and magnificent landscape make it a thrilling experience for water sports aficionados. The

island of Sardinia, notably Porto Pollo, and Punta Trettu provides great conditions for both windsurfing and kitesurfing. The seaside cities of Tarifa and Cagliari are other popular locations for these adrenaline-pumping activities.

4. **Stand-Up Paddleboarding**: Stand-up paddleboarding (SUP) has acquired enormous popularity in recent years, and Italy's coastal districts give wonderful settings to enjoy this pastime. The tranquil waters of Lake Como and Lake Garda are great for SUP, where you can paddle between magnificent scenery and lovely villages. Along the Italian Riviera, you may kayak along the shore and discover secret coves and caves. SUP is also a terrific way to explore the crystal-clear seas of Sicily's coastline, with its picturesque beaches and towering cliffs.

5. **Kayaking and Canoeing**: Italy's coastal areas provide different chances for kayaking and canoeing, enabling you to explore the magnificent coastline and find hidden jewels. The Venice Lagoon gives a unique kayaking experience, where you may paddle among the canals and view the city's ancient architecture. The Gulf of Naples, with its blue seas, gives the possibility to kayak around the famed island of

Capri. The Cinque Terre National Park on the Italian Riviera is another famous place for kayaking, where you can paddle among the colorful fishing towns tucked between cliffs.

6. **Jet Skiing and Water Skiing**: For those seeking high-speed thrills on the water, jet skiing and wave skiing are popular alternatives along Italy's coastline. The Italian Riviera, Amalfi Coast, and Sardinia's Costa Smeralda are recognized for their jet ski rental services, enabling you to explore the gorgeous surroundings while having an adrenaline-pumping ride. Water skiing is also offered in numerous coastal places, offering an exciting feeling as you float through the water.

Before partaking in any water sports activity, it's necessary to emphasize safety. Be cautious to observe local restrictions, wear adequate safety gear, and consider taking classes or hiring professional guides, particularly if you're new to a specific activity.

Embrace the splendor of Italy's shoreline and delve into the diversity of water sports activities offered. Whether you're an experienced enthusiast or a novice, the coastal areas of Italy offer something for everyone, offering amazing experiences and lasting memories.

- Skiing in the Italian Alps

The Italian Alps provide a winter paradise for skiing fans with its beautiful scenery, outstanding ski resorts, and rich cultural legacy. Nestled in the northern section of Italy, the Alps span over various areas, including Aosta Valley, Lombardy, Trentino-Alto Adige, and Veneto. With its snowy peaks, beautiful slopes, and attractive mountain communities, the Italian Alps give a unique and spectacular skiing experience for novices and seasoned skiers alike.

Ski Resorts in the Italian Alps:

The Italian Alps have an incredible selection of ski resorts that cater to all levels of skiing experience. Here are some of the most recognized ski locations in the region:

1. **Cortina d'Ampezzo**: Located in the Dolomites, Cortina d'Ampezzo is one of the most glamorous ski resorts in the world. It has hosted the Winter Olympics and provides a blend of tough slopes, breathtaking scenery, and a dynamic après-ski culture.

2. **Val Gardena**: Situated in the heart of the Dolomites, Val Gardena is a popular destination for skiers and snowboarders. Its interconnecting

slopes allow access to nearly 175 kilometers of groomed lines, with stunning views of the surrounding mountain peaks.

3. **Madonna di Campiglio**: Nestled in the Brenta Dolomites, Madonna di Campiglio is noted for its elegant environment and outstanding skiing conditions. It has a massive ski region with over 150 kilometers of slopes, including the famed "3-Tre" slope, which holds the FIS Alpine Ski World Cup competitions.

4. **Sestriere**: As part of the Via Lattea ski resort, Sestriere is a known destination for winter sports aficionados. It acquired worldwide renown as the venue of the alpine skiing events at the 2006 Winter Olympics and provides a broad choice of slopes for all ability levels.

5. **Cervinia**: Situated in the Valle d'Aosta region, Cervinia is notable for its huge ski area and its proximity to the Swiss resort of Zermatt. Skiers may enjoy stunning views of the renowned Matterhorn while exploring over 350 kilometers of terrain.

Skiing Conditions and Season:

The skiing season in the Italian Alps normally runs from late November to April, however, this may vary depending on snowfall and weather conditions. Higher-altitude resorts tend to enjoy longer seasons, with some remaining open until early May. The Alps get sufficient snowfall, giving great skiing conditions throughout the winter months.

The Italian Alps provide a broad selection of slopes appropriate for skiers of all levels. From easy beginning slopes to tough off-piste terrain, there is something for everyone. Ski schools and instructors are available at most slopes to assist novices get started or enhance the abilities of more experienced skiers.

Beyond Skiing: Winter Activities and Cultural Experiences:

While skiing is the primary draw in the Italian Alps, there are plenty of other activities and cultural events to enjoy during your stay. Here are a few highlights:

1. **Snowboarding and Freestyle Parks**: Many resorts in the Italian Alps offer specialized snowboarding parks and freestyle zones featuring jumps, rails, and halfpipes. These facilities appeal to snowboarders and freestyle skiers eager to demonstrate their talents and stunts.

2. **Snowshoeing and Winter Hiking**: Explore the beautiful alpine vistas on foot by taking part in snowshoeing or winter hiking tours. These

activities give a fresh view of the mountains, enabling you to immerse yourself in the peacefulness of the winter environment.

3. **Spa and Wellness**: After an intense day on the slopes, rest and refresh at one of the region's spa and wellness facilities. Many resorts provide excellent spa facilities where you may luxuriate in massages, saunas, hot tubs, and other health services.

4. **Gastronomy & Apres-Ski**: The Italian Alps are known for their gastronomic pleasures. Enjoy classic alpine meals such as polenta, fondue, and substantial stews in warm mountain chalets and attractive eateries. After a day of skiing, relax with a hot drink or aperitif at one of the vibrant apres-ski pubs.

5. **Cultural Explorations**: The Italian Alps are deep in history and culture. Explore lovely alpine communities, explore old castles, and learn about the local traditions and customs. The region's rich tradition offers added depth to your skiing experience.

Practical Information:

- **Getting there**: The Italian Alps are well-connected by airports, with major gateways including Milan, Turin, Verona, and

Venice. From the airports, you may easily reach the ski resorts by rail, bus, or private service.

- **lodging**: The ski resorts in the Italian Alps provide a broad choice of lodging alternatives, from luxury hotels and chalets to quaint guest houses and flats. It's important to book in advance, particularly during the high season.

- **Equipment Rental**: If you don't have your skiing gear, most mountains offer rental stores where you may lease skis, boots, and other equipment. Professional personnel can help you in obtaining the proper gear for your requirements.

- **Safety**: While skiing, it's crucial to observe safety requirements, wear suitable protective gear, and be aware of your surroundings. Check weather and avalanche conditions often and ski within your skill level.

- **Ski Passes**: Most resorts provide ski passes that give access to the whole ski region. These passes may be bought for varied lengths, from a single day to a week or more, depending on your length of stay and skiing objectives.

In conclusion, Skiing in the Italian Alps is a dream come true for winter sports fans. From the breathtaking mountain scenery to the world-class ski resorts and the distinct cultural experiences, the Italian Alps deliver an unparalleled skiing journey. Whether you are a novice or an experienced skier, the Italian Alps offer a broad choice of slopes, good snow conditions, and a warm and inviting ambiance. So grab your skis or snowboard and get ready to enjoy the adrenaline and beauty of skiing in the Italian Alps!

- Sailing in the Mediterranean

Sailing in the Mediterranean is a dream come true for many sailing lovers, and Italy provides a thrilling and varied experience for those wishing to explore its magnificent beaches. With its rich history, breathtaking scenery, and lively culture, Italy offers a superb setting for a sailing trip. Whether you're an expert sailor or a beginner seeking to try something new, the Mediterranean in Italy provides a plethora of chances for a fantastic sailing experience. In this thorough guide, we'll cover all you need to know about sailing on the Mediterranean in Italy.

1. **Geographical Overview**: Italy is situated in Southern Europe and is flanked by the Mediterranean Sea on three sides—the Adriatic

Sea to the east, the Ionian Sea to the south, and the Tyrrhenian Sea to the west. The Italian coastline covers over 7,600 kilometers, boasting scenic islands, sandy beaches, craggy cliffs, and lovely coastal villages.

2. **Sailing sites**: Italy provides numerous famous sailing sites in the Mediterranean, each giving its particular charm and attractions. Some of the popular locations include:

- **Amalfi Coast**: Known for its stunning cliffs, bustling coastal towns like Positano and Amalfi, and attractive anchorages, the coast of Amalfi, Italy is a must-visit for sailors seeking natural beauty and cultural experiences.

- **Sardinia**: This vast Italian island in the Tyrrhenian Sea has crystal-clear seas, clean beaches, and spectacular rock formations, making it a haven for sailing aficionados. The Costa Smeralda, with its spectacular ports and opulent resorts, is a favorite place for yacht chartering.

- **Sicily**: The biggest island in the Mediterranean, Sicily, provides a broad selection of sailing adventures. From visiting the lively metropolis of Palermo to finding hidden coves and the UNESCO World Heritage site of the Aeolian Islands, Sicily offers something for everyone.

- **Tuscan Archipelago**: Located in the Tyrrhenian Sea, the Tuscan Archipelago encompasses seven principal islands, including Elba, Giglio, and Capraia. It's a paradise for nature lovers, with its crystal-clear oceans, marine parks, and unspoiled landscapes.

- **Italian Riviera**: Stretching along the northwestern coast, the Italian Riviera is famed for its picturesque beach villages, such as Portofino and Cinque Terre. Sailing along this coast provides a great combination of culture, gastronomy, and magnificent landscapes.

3. **Sailing Seasons**: The Mediterranean environment in Italy allows for sailing excursions throughout the year, but the ideal season to sail is during the spring (April to June) and autumn (September to October) when the weather is good, and the crowds are fewer. Summer (July to August) is attractive but may be rather hot and congested in tourist places. Winter sailing is less prevalent but may still be pleasant in warmer places like Sicily and Sardinia.

4. **Nautical Infrastructure**: Italy has a well-developed nautical infrastructure with various marinas, ports, and anchorages along its coastline. Major cities and coastal towns provide marinas outfitted with facilities such as fuel stations, power, water supply, and maintenance services. It's essential to make reservations in advance, particularly during high season, to assure a spot at your selected marina.

5. **Sailing legislation**: When sailing in Italy, it's crucial to conform to local legislation and have the proper paperwork. Non-European Union sailors should have a valid passport and may need a visa, depending on their nationality. Additionally, sailors must have boat registration documentation, insurance certificates, and personal identification. Familiarize yourself with navigation regulations, local limits, and the VHF channel system to guarantee a safe and compliant sailing experience.

6. **Chartering Options**: For individuals who don't possess a boat, chartering is a popular choice to explore the Mediterranean in Italy. Numerous charter businesses are providing a large selection of sailing yachts, catamarans, and motorboats for hire. Popular charter bases are found in large cities and seaside towns like

Naples, Palermo, and Olbia. Hiring a professional captain or crew is also feasible if you want a more relaxing and supervised sailing experience.

7. **Sailing Itineraries**: Italy provides a choice of sailing itineraries responding to varied interests and lengths. Here are a few recommended paths to consider:

- **Amalfi Coast and Capri**: Explore the magnificent Amalfi Coast, visit the luxurious island of Capri, and explore lovely cities like Sorrento, Positano, and Amalfi.

- **Aeolian Islands**: Set sail from Sicily and tour the spectacular Aeolian Islands, including Lipari, Stromboli, and Panarea. Experience volcanic scenery, hot springs, and gorgeous beaches.

- **Tuscan Archipelago**: Start from the mainland or Elba Island and visit the gorgeous islands of the Tuscan Archipelago, including Giglio, Giannutri, and Montecristo.

- **Sardinian Coastline**: Embark on a voyage down the coast of Sardinia, visiting the famed Costa Smeralda, Maddalena Archipelago, and the pristine beauty of the southern shore.

8. **Local Cuisine and Culture**: Sailing in Italy gives you the ideal chance to enjoy the country's gastronomic pleasures and immerse yourself in its colorful culture. Each area has its gastronomic specialties, such as pizza in Naples, fresh seafood in Sicily, and superb wines in Tuscany. Exploring seaside towns enables you to discover local customs, explore historical monuments, and appreciate the wonderful friendliness of the Italian people.

9. **Must-See sights**: Apart from the wonderful sailing experience, Italy provides a profusion of must-see sights that are conveniently accessible from the shore. Consider experiencing renowned locations like the Colosseum in Rome, the ancient city of Pompeii, the charming city of Florence, and the archaeological sites of Sicily, including the Valley of the Temples.

10. **Safety Considerations**: While sailing in the Mediterranean in Italy is typically safe, it's necessary to keep educated about weather conditions, pay attention to navigational risks, and observe safety standards. Keep a watch on weather predictions and be prepared for occasional severe gusts, particularly in select places like the Strait of Bonifacio. Ensure you

have adequate safety equipment on board, including life jackets, flares, and a first aid pack.

Sailing in the Mediterranean in Italy provides a mesmerizing combination of natural beauty, cultural richness, and remarkable experiences. Whether you want to lease a boat or bring your own, this wonderful area provides a sailing vacation packed with stunning panoramas, secret coves, great food, and warm Italian hospitality. Embark on a voyage across Italy's coastline treasures and make lifetime memories as you cruise the Mediterranean waters.

CHAPTER 8. Traveling on a Budget

- Cost-Saving Tips

Italy is a gorgeous and culturally rich nation famed for its ancient sites, great food, and magnificent scenery. While it provides wonderful experiences for tourists, it's also crucial to keep an eye on your budget to get the most out of your vacation. Here are some ways to cut expenses to help you enjoy Italy without breaking the bank:

1. **Travel during the shoulder seasons**: Italy's main tourist season is during the summer months, especially in major sites like Rome, Florence, and Venice. By visiting during the shoulder seasons of spring (April-May) and fall (September-October), you may escape the crowds and enjoy better pricing on lodgings, airlines, and activities.

2. **Opt for cheap lodgings**: Instead of spending on luxury hotels, try staying in budget-friendly accommodations such as hostels, guesthouses, or bed & breakfasts. These choices are not only cheaper but may also give a more genuine

experience, enabling you to engage with locals and other visitors.

3. **Use public transit**: Italy has a vast and efficient public transportation system, including trains and buses. Instead of depending on taxis or private transport, utilize public transit to go about. Trains, in particular, are a quick and economical means to travel between cities, with regional trains providing reduced tickets compared to high-speed trains.

4. **Enjoy street food and local markets**: Italian cuisine is recognized internationally, and you may taste its delights without necessarily eating in pricey places. Opt for street food like pizza by the slice, paninis, or gelato from local sellers. Additionally, explore local markets where you can purchase fresh vegetables, cheese, and cured meats for a picnic-style supper at a fraction of the cost.

5. **Take advantage of free attractions**: Italy is home to several free attractions that enable you to immerse yourself in its rich history and culture. Many churches, including St. Peter's Basilica in Vatican City or Basilica di Santa Maria del Fiore in Florence, are free to visit. Explore public spaces, such as Piazza Navona

in Rome or Piazza del Campo in Siena, to take in the ambiance without spending a penny.

6. **Pack a refillable water bottle**: Bottled water may be pricey, particularly in popular places. Carry a refillable water bottle and make use of the numerous public fountains sprinkled around Italian cities. Tap water in Italy is typically safe to drink, so you can remain hydrated without spending money on bottled water.

7. **Eat where the locals eat**: Avoid eateries situated near big tourist sites since they tend to be more costly. Instead, wander into the side streets and hunt for modest trattorias or osterias where residents eat. These eateries frequently serve genuine Italian cuisine at lesser pricing.

8. **Plan museum visits strategically**: Italy is home to several world-class museums and art galleries. Many of them provide free or reduced entry on specified days or during certain hours. Research the museums you wish to visit and take advantage of these options to save money while still experiencing the cultural riches Italy has to offer.

9. **Use local SIM cards or Wi-Fi**: Avoid exorbitant roaming costs by acquiring a local SIM card for your phone. This enables you to make calls, utilize data, and access the internet

at local prices. Alternatively, make use of free Wi-Fi hotspots offered in cafés, restaurants, and public locations to remain connected without paying extra fees.

10. **Be careful of tourist traps**: While touring major tourist attractions, be wary of tourist traps that may overcharge for services or goods. Research and read reviews before making any purchases or arranging activities to verify you're receiving a fair deal.

By following these cost-saving strategies, you may enjoy the best of Italy while keeping your spending in control. Remember, it's frequently the basic and honest moments that create a vacation special, so embrace the local culture and enjoy your time touring this beautiful nation without breaking your wallet.

- Affordable Accommodation

When planning a vacation to Italy, choosing economical lodging is an important component of your travel plans. Italy is a renowned tourist destination recognized for its rich history, breathtaking architecture, great food, and lovely scenery. Fortunately, there are different alternatives available for economical lodging around the nation, ranging from budget hotels to guesthouses, hostels, and vacation rentals. This detailed material will walk you through the many forms of budget lodging in Italy and give important ideas to help you locate the right location to stay without breaking the bank.

1. **Budget Hotels**: Budget hotels are a popular alternative for visitors seeking economical lodging in Italy. These motels often provide minimal facilities, pleasant accommodations, and handy locations. While they may not give the same degree of luxury as higher-end hotels, they frequently provide exceptional value for money. Some well-known cheap hotel chains in Italy are Hotel Ibis, Hotel Formule 1, and Hotel Première Classe. You may discover affordable hotels in both large cities and smaller communities around the nation.

2. **Guesthouses**: Guesthouses, commonly known as bed and breakfasts (B&Bs), are another economical lodging choice in Italy. These places are often smaller than hotels and provide a more intimate and friendly feel. Guesthouses frequently give pleasant rooms with private or communal toilets along with breakfast in the lodging charge. They are an excellent choice for those who prefer a personal

touch and wish to experience the local culture. Websites like Airbnb and Booking.com provide a large selection of guesthouses and B&Bs around Italy.

3. **Hostels**: If you're a budget-conscious tourist or a solitary traveler wishing to meet other travelers, hostels are a terrific alternative. Italy has a strong hostel sector, especially in large cities and important tourist sites. Hostels provide dormitory-style housing with shared amenities such as kitchens, baths, and common spaces. Some hostels also give private rooms for people desiring additional solitude. Staying at a hostel not only helps you save money but also gives you a chance to network and connect with other like-minded travelers.

4. **Agriturismos**: For a unique and economical accommodation experience in rural Italy, try staying at an agriturismo. Agriturismos are functioning farms or rural estates that provide visitor lodgings. These facilities give a chance to immerse oneself in the countryside, taste traditional farm-to-table meals, and experience local agricultural activities. Agriturismos vary from basic rooms to more elegant suites, and many provide facilities like swimming pools, onsite restaurants, and guided excursions. It's

good to hire a vehicle while staying at an agriturismo to explore the nearby regions.

5. **Vacation Rentals**: Vacation rentals, such as apartments, villas, or homes, are a popular alternative for families or bigger groups vacationing together. Renting a vacation home enables you to have more room, freedom, and the chance to make your meals, which may help save money on eating out. Websites like Airbnb, HomeAway, and VRBO provide a large range of holiday rentals around Italy, catering to all budgets and interests. It's vital to read reviews, examine the property's location, and connect with the host before making a booking.

Tips for Finding Affordable Accommodation in Italy:

- **Book in advance**: Prices for lodging tend to climb as the trip date approaches. Booking your hotel early in advance might help you achieve better pricing and availability.

- **Consider seasonal travel**: Visiting Italy during the winter months (spring or autumn) may typically result in reduced accommodation charges compared to the peak tourist season (summer). Additionally, you'll meet fewer crowds, making your trip more pleasurable.

- **Research various regions**: Accommodation rates might vary greatly depending on the area in Italy. Consider visiting less touristic places or smaller towns where rates may be more inexpensive.

- **Compare prices**: Utilize online channels, such as hotel comparison websites or vacation rental platforms, to compare costs and discover the best bargains. Don't forget to examine the reviews and ratings of the hotels before making a selection.

- **Stay outside city centers**: Accommodation costs in city centers are often higher. Consider staying in surrounding suburbs or areas linked to the city core via public transit. In this manner, you may save money while still having convenient access to the key attractions.

- **Take advantage of discounts and promotions**: Keep an eye out for special deals, savings for longer stays, or loyalty programs given by hotels or booking sites. These might assist you to save money on your hotel expenditures.

In conclusion, finding economical lodging in Italy is achievable with a little study and effort. Whether you select a cheap hotel, guesthouse, hostel, agriturismo, or vacation rental, there are alternatives to fit every budget and travel style. By following the ideas presented and touring different places, you can make your Italian vacation both memorable and budget-friendly.

- Cheap Eats and Local Markets

Italy is famous for its rich culinary past, and visiting the country's affordable meals and local markets is a fantastic opportunity to explore its different tastes and lively food culture. From lively street food booths to traditional markets loaded with fresh fruit, Italy provides a multitude of economical eating alternatives that are both tasty and genuine. In this post, we'll dig into the world of inexpensive meals and local markets in Italy, showcasing some popular dishes and must-visit destinations for food fans.

Cheap Eats in Italy:

Italy is home to a vast assortment of economical and exquisite cuisine that won't break the purse. Whether you're wandering through the cobblestone streets of Rome or trekking into the picturesque lanes of Florence, you'll discover several alternatives for affordable food that suit both your taste buds and your pocketbook. Here are some common choices:

1. **Pizza al Taglio**: This Roman specialty is a terrific alternative for a fast and economical supper. Pizza al taglio, or "pizza by the slice," is offered in rectangular slices and includes a range of toppings. You may find these appealing pizza restaurants around the nation, where you pay by the weight of the slice you pick.

2. **Panini**: Italians are famed for their expertise in sandwich-making, and panini is a good example. These grilled sandwiches are often constructed with fresh ingredients such as cured meats, cheeses, and vegetables, all packed between two layers of crusty bread. Look for tiny delis or street sellers providing a selection of panini alternatives.

3. **Tramezzini**: Tramezzini are triangular, crustless sandwiches that are popular in Venice. These wonderful finger sandwiches are created with soft, white bread and filled with diverse components including tuna, ham, cheese, and veggies. Tramezzini are typically offered in pubs and cafés as a fast snack or light lunch alternative.

4. **Pasta**: Pasta is a mainstay of Italian cuisine and is offered at inexpensive pricing in

many eateries around the nation. Look for local trattorias or osterias that serve pasta meals cooked with simple, tasty sauces like aglio e olio (garlic and olive oil) or Pomodoro (tomato sauce).

5. **Gelato**: No vacation to Italy is complete without indulging in some gelato. This creamy and delightful frozen dessert is available in various gelaterias, and you may frequently find cheap choices. Look for establishments where residents queue up since they tend to serve high-quality gelato at moderate pricing.

Local Markets in Italy:

Exploring local markets in Italy is an immersive experience that enables you to observe the brilliant colors, seductive fragrances, and busy atmosphere that are typical of Italian culinary culture. These markets give a chance to connect with local sellers, explore fresh vegetables, and uncover uncommon products. Here are a few prominent marketplaces in Italy:

1. **Mercato di Porta Palazzo (Turin)**: Located in Turin, this is one of the biggest open-air marketplaces in Europe. It provides a vast choice of items, including fruits, vegetables, meats, cheeses, and local specialties. The market also has vendors

offering apparel, antiques, and household products.

2. **Mercato di San Lorenzo (Florence)**: Situated near the Basilica of San Lorenzo, this market is a delight for food lovers. It provides a broad range of items, including fresh fruit, cured meats, cheeses, olive oil, truffles, and wine. You may also discover handicrafts, leather products, and souvenirs.

3. **Mercato di Rialto (Venice)**: Located near the renowned Rialto Bridge, this market has been a lively commercial center for generations. It provides a varied choice of seafood, fruits, veggies, spices, and local items. The market is a wonderful spot to enjoy the flavors of Venetian food and watch the Venetian way of life.

4. **Mercato Centrale (Florence)**: Situated in a beautifully renovated 19th-century structure, Mercato Centrale is a dynamic food market that provides a broad range of local and foreign delicacies. It contains kiosks with fresh fruit, meats, cheeses, pastries, and street food merchants offering up tasty nibbles.

5. **Mercato di Testaccio (Rome)**: Located in the Testaccio area, this market is famous among residents for its fresh fruit, meats, and

regional delicacies. It's an excellent spot to experience classic Roman street cuisine including supplì (rice balls), porchetta (roast pig), and artisanal cheeses.

Visiting these local markets not only allows uncovering the freshest products but also offers an insight into the everyday lives of Italians as they go about their culinary routines. Be sure to explore early in the morning when the markets are at their liveliest and when the fruit is at its freshest.

In conclusion, visiting inexpensive eats and local markets in Italy is a wonderful opportunity to immerse oneself in the country's culinary culture while enjoying tasty and economical meals. From enjoying scrumptious slices of pizza al Taglio to visiting the colorful booths of busy markets, you'll discover an assortment of gastronomic pleasures that demonstrate the richness of Italian cuisine. So, don't miss the opportunity to indulge in these economical gourmet adventures and appreciate the flavors of Italy. Buon appetito!

- Free Attractions and Activities

Italy is a nation recognized for its rich history, gorgeous scenery, and lively culture. While it's true that Italy provides lots of outstanding sights and experiences that come with a price tag, countless free attractions and activities enable tourists to explore and enjoy the nation without paying a dollar. Whether you're an economical visitor or just searching for unique experiences off the usual route, here is a thorough guide to free sites and activities in Italy.

1. **Explore Historic buildings and Monuments**: Italy is home to an astonishing number of historic buildings and monuments that give free admission or have designated free entrance days. Some significant instances include:

- **Roman Forum and Palatine Hill in Rome**: On the first Sunday of every month, you may explore these historic sites for free.

- **Colosseum in Rome**: Although access to the Colosseum itself needs a ticket, you may experience its magnificence from the outside without paying a dime.

- **Pompeii Archaeological Site**: Located near Naples, Pompeii is a massive archaeological site that may be toured for free on the first Sunday of the month.

- **Pantheon in Rome**: This ancient Roman temple is open to explore and is a wonderful architectural masterpiece.

2. **Wander through Charming Towns and Villages**: Italy is studded with lovely towns and villages that ooze charm and create a great setting for leisurely excursions. Some of the most stunning and free-to-explore sites include:

- **Cinque Terre**: This cluster of colorful fishing towns on the Italian Riviera provides spectacular coastline scenery and hiking trails, with some pathways accessible without charge.

- **Assisi**: Known for its link to St. Francis, Assisi is a hilltop town in Umbria that has tiny alleyways, antique buildings, and spectacular vistas.

- **San Gimignano**: Famous for its medieval towers, San Gimignano in Tuscany is a UNESCO World Heritage Site with a well-preserved old core.

- **Matera**: Located in southern Italy, Matera is noted for its unusual cave houses and historic Sassi neighborhoods, which may be freely explored on foot.

3. **Enjoy Free Museums and Art Galleries**: Several museums and art galleries in Italy provide free entrance, either permanently or on special days. Some of the major possibilities include:

- **Vatican Museums in Rome**: On the last Sunday of every month, the Vatican Museums, including the awe-inspiring Sistine Chapel, may be seen for free.

- **National Roman Museum in Rome**: This museum holds an enormous collection of ancient Roman antiquities and gives free admittance on the first Sunday of each month.

- **Uffizi Gallery in Florence**: While ordinary entrance to the Uffizi Gallery costs a ticket, on the first Sunday of every month, you may attend for free and view Renaissance masterpieces.

- **Pinacoteca di Brera in Milan**: This art gallery is free to visit every Tuesday afternoon, offering it a wonderful chance to examine its collection of Italian Renaissance art.

4. **Discover Natural Beauty**: Italy's natural landscapes are as varied as they are magnificent, and many of them may be appreciated without spending any money. Here are a few examples:

- **Lake Como**: Surrounded by mountains and attractive villages, Lake Como provides breathtaking panoramas and possibilities for lakeside walks.

- **Amalfi Coast**: While certain activities along the Amalfi Coast cost money, you may still enjoy the spectacular views by just walking along the coastal roads or exploring the adjacent trails.

- **Gran Paradiso National Park**: Located in the Alps, this national park provides fantastic trekking options, with varied animals and spectacular alpine landscapes.

- **Stroll through Public Gardens**: Many Italian towns, like Rome, Florence, and Venice, feature wonderful public gardens where you can relax, enjoy the view, and have a picnic.

5. **Explore Local Culture and Festivals**: Immersing yourself in the local culture is a terrific way to explore Italy without spending much. Keep a watch out for free events, festivals, and cultural activities occurring during your stay. Some towns are especially noted for their dynamic atmospheres and frequent free events, like Naples with its street performances and Palermo with its traditional markets and boisterous street festivals.

6. Take Advantage of Free Walking Tours: Numerous cities in Italy offer free walking tours conducted by professional guides who give insights into the history, culture, and hidden jewels of the region. While these excursions are officially free, it's common to pay the guide at the conclusion if you appreciated the experience. This is a fantastic opportunity to tour the city, discover intriguing tales, and obtain suggestions for additional free activities.

Remember, even if some sites and activities are free, it's always a good idea to check their opening hours, availability, and any possible limitations before organizing your visit. With this complete book, you can now go on a budget-friendly journey, exploring the beauty and culture of Italy without breaking the bank.

- Transportation Savings

Italy, recognized for its rich history, lively culture, and gorgeous landscapes, provides countless options for tourists to enjoy its treasures. When planning a vacation to Italy, it's crucial to consider transportation expenditures, since they may considerably affect your whole budget. Fortunately, there are different methods to save money on transportation while enjoying everything that Italy has to offer. In this post, we will discuss several efficient techniques for transportation savings in Italy.

1. **Public Transportation**: Italy features a large and efficient public transportation infrastructure, giving it another economical and handy alternative for tourists. Cities like Rome, Milan, Florence, and Naples have well-developed networks of buses, trams, and metros that can transport you to key sites and districts. Consider buying multi-day or weekly passes, such as the Roma Pass in Rome or the Carta Agile in Milan, which give unlimited rides at a subsidized price. These permits typically provide extra perks, such as free access to museums and discounts on tourist sites.

2. **Regional Trains**: Traveling between cities in Italy may be pricey, particularly if you depend only on high-speed trains. However, regional trains give a cheaper option for shorter distances. These trains may take somewhat longer, but they provide stunning vistas of the countryside and enable you to enjoy the unique charm of little villages along the route. Check the Trenitalia website for regional train

timetables and rates, and consider reserving in advance to ensure the best discounts.

3. **Carpooling and Ride-Sharing**: If you're traveling with a group or prefer the flexibility of private transportation, carpooling and ride-sharing services may help you save money. Platforms like BlaBlaCar and Uber are accessible in many Italian cities and provide shared trips at a fraction of the cost of regular taxis. Additionally, carpooling enables you to meet and connect with locals or other visitors, increasing your whole experience.

4. **Bike Rentals**: Exploring Italian towns on a bicycle may be both cost-effective and pleasant. Many cities, including Rome, Florence, and Milan, offer bike-sharing systems that enable you to borrow bicycles for short periods at inexpensive prices. This eco-friendly means of transportation not only saves you money but also gives a unique viewpoint as you travel through the picturesque streets and attractions of Italy.

5. **Walking**: One of the easiest methods to save money on transportation in Italy is by just walking. Italy's cities are frequently small and pedestrian-friendly, making walking a perfect alternative for discovering local neighborhoods

and sights. Walking not only saves you money but also enables you to immerse yourself in the colorful environment, uncover hidden jewels, and experience the real spirit of Italian culture.

6. **Off-Peak Travel**: Consider organizing your vacations to Italy during off-peak seasons or weekdays, since transportation rates tend to be cheaper during these periods. Avoiding major holidays and busy tourist times may drastically lower expenses for flights, trains, and lodgings. Additionally, attractions and famous locations are frequently less crowded, enabling you to enjoy them more comfortably.

7. **Research and Compare costs**: Before making any transportation arrangements, undertake comprehensive research and compare costs from multiple suppliers. Airlines, railway companies, and bus services in Italy typically have varied ticket systems and promotional offers. Utilize internet travel services, such as Skyscanner or Rome2rio, to compare costs and identify the most cost-effective solutions. Flexibility with travel dates and timings might also help you locate better bargains.

8. **Travel Passes and City Cards**: Several travel passes and city cards are available in Italy that give bundled savings on transportation,

attractions, and services. For example, the Italy Rail Pass gives unlimited rail travel for a fixed number of days during a predetermined time. City-specific cards, such as the Firenze Card in Florence or the Venezia Unica in Venice, give free or subsidized entry to various destinations and include public transit advantages.

9. **Plan Efficient Routes**: Planning your route to reduce needless travel will save you both time and money. Research the vicinity of attractions and organize your trips appropriately to minimize unnecessary commuting. By combining neighboring sites, you may save transportation expenditures and optimize your time spent experiencing the locations.

10. **Stay Close to Transportation Hubs**: When picking lodgings, choose hotels or guesthouses that are conveniently placed near transportation hubs, such as railway stations or bus terminals. This helps you to save money on taxis or other transportation expenditures while going to and from your resort. Moreover, residing near transit hubs allows quick access to public transportation, making it more convenient to explore the city.

By applying these transportation savings tactics in Italy, you can make the most of your vacation while keeping your budget in control. Whether you pick public transportation, regional trains, carpooling, bicycling, or walking, each choice provides distinct benefits and cost-saving potential. Plan, check costs, and consider off-peak travel to guarantee an enjoyable and economical Italian experience.

CHAPTER 9. Language and Travel Resources

- Useful Italian Phrases

Greetings and Basic Phrases:
1. Ciao! - Hello!/Goodbye!
2. Buongiorno! - Good morning!/Good day!
3. Buonasera! - Good evening!
4. Buonanotte! - Good night!
5. Come stai? - How are you?
6. Sto bene, grazie. E tu? - I'm alright, thank you. And you?
7. Mi chiamo [name]. - My name is [name].
8. Piacere di concerti. - Nice to meet you.
9. Scusa/Scusami - Excuse me/sorry (informal)
10. Per favore - Please
11. Grazie - Thank you
12. Prego - You're welcome
13. Mi dispiace - I'm sorry

Introductions and Small Talk:
14. Da dove vieni? - Where are you from? (to a stranger)
15. Sono di [country]. - I am from [country].
16. Che lavoro fai? - What do you do for a living?
17. Mi piace molto l'Italia. - I enjoy Italy.

18. Hai dei piani per stasera? - Do you have any plans for tonight?

Ordering Food and Drinks:

19. Vorrei un caffè, per favore. - I would like a coffee, please.

20. Mi piacerebbe mangiare la pizza Margherita. - I would like to eat Margherita pizza.

21. Il conto, per favore. - The bill, please.

22. Avete un menù in inglese? - Do you have an English menu?

Asking for Directions:

23. Mi scusi, dove si trova [place]? - Excuse me, where is [place]?

24. È lontano? - Is it far?

25. A Destra - To the right

26. A sinistra - To the left

27. Avanti - Straightforward

28. Grazie per l'aiuto. - Thank you for your assistance.

Shopping:

29. Quanto Costa? - How much does it cost?

30. Posso provarlo? - Can I try it on?

31. Mi piace, lo prendo. - I like it, I'll take it.

32. Accettate carte di credito? - Do you take credit cards?

Emergencies:

33. Aiuto! - Help!

34. Ho bisogno di un dottore. - I need a doctor.

35. Chiamate la Polizia! - Call the cops!

Transportation:

36. Vorrei un biglietto per [destination], per favore. - I would like a ticket to [place], please.

37. A che ora parte il treno/autobus? - What time does the train/bus leave?

38. Quanto dura il viaggio? - How long does the travel take?

39. Dove posso prendere un taxi? - Where can I obtain a taxi?

Numbers:

40. Uno, due, tre, quattro, cinque - One, two, three, four, five

41. Dieci, venti, trenta, Quaranta, cinquanta - Ten, twenty, thirty, forty, fifty

42. Cento, mille - One hundred, one thousand

Miscellaneous:

43. Mi piace molto! - I like it a lot!

44. Non Capisco. - I don't understand.

45. Che bello! - How beautiful/nice!

46. Auguri! - Best wishes!

47. Buon viaggio! - Have a pleasant vacation!

Remember, repetition and immersion in the language are crucial to becoming more proficient and comfortable with these words. Enjoy studying Italian!

- Travel Apps and Websites

When planning a vacation to Italy, it's useful to harness technology to improve your travel experience. Whether you need to book lodgings, identify local sights, use public transit, or discover the finest restaurants, there are various travel applications and websites particularly made for Italy. Here's a thorough selection of handy travel applications and websites to assist you throughout your visit:

1. **Rome2rio (Website/App)** - Rome2rio helps you organize your travel by offering thorough information on numerous transportation alternatives, including airlines, trains, buses, and ferries. It also displays predicted trip times and expenses for various routes.

2. **Skyscanner (Website/App)** - Skyscanner enables you to search for and compare flights to and from Italy. It gives extensive flight information, including prices, airlines, and

departure/arrival times, helping you locate the best discounts.

3. **Trenitalia (Website/App)** - Trenitalia is the official website and app for Italy's national train operator. You may use it to look for train timetables, purchase tickets, and check platform information. It covers both regional and long-distance rail services.

4. **Italo (Website/App)** - Italo is a privately-owned high-speed rail service in Italy. Their website and app allow you to look for train connections, purchase tickets, and manage your reservations on their contemporary and luxurious trains.

5. **Moovit (App)** - Moovit is a comprehensive public transportation app that helps you navigate Italy's cities by offering real-time bus, tram, and subway information. It includes extensive route planning, actual departure schedules, and even notifications for service delays.

6. **Google Maps (App)** - Google Maps is an amazing tool for finding your way around Italy. It gives precise maps, turn-by-turn instructions, and real-time traffic information. It also gives public transit information for major cities.

7. **TripAdvisor (Website/App)** - TripAdvisor is a popular platform for seeking travel information, suggestions, and reviews. It may help you find activities, restaurants, and lodgings in Italy, sharing perspectives with other visitors.

8. **Eatigo (App)** - Eatigo provides discounts on eating experiences in Italy. The app enables you to browse restaurants, check available deals, and book reservations. It's a terrific choice for locating and reserving meals at a cheap price.

9. **HappyCow (Website/App)** - HappyCow is a helpful resource for vegetarian and vegan travelers. It helps you identify vegetarian and vegan-friendly restaurants, cafés, and businesses around Italy, giving reviews and ratings from the community.

10. **Musement (Website/App)** - Musement provides a choice of tailored tours, activities, and experiences throughout Italy. You may use the website or app to explore and schedule guided tours, skip-the-line tickets to major sights, and unique local experiences

11. **XE Currency (software)** - XE Currency is a reputable currency converter software that enables you to rapidly check the exchange rates between various currencies. It might be

beneficial for budgeting and understanding the worth of products and services in Italy.

12. **TIM Wi-Fi (App)** - TIM Wi-Fi is an app that lets you discover Wi-Fi connections across Italy. It enables you to connect to TIM's large network of public Wi-Fi sites, enabling you to remain connected throughout your travels.

13. **MyTaxi (App)** - MyTaxi (currently named FREE currently) is a popular app for booking cabs in major Italian cities. It enables you to order a cab, monitor its whereabouts, and pay securely using the smartphone.

14. **Rentalcars.com (Website/App)** - Rentalcars.com is a website for booking rental cars in Italy. You may compare costs from several rental providers, pick the finest automobile for your requirements, and make reservations in advance

15. **Airbnb (Website/App)** - Airbnb is a well-known platform for reserving lodgings globally, including in Italy. It provides a broad variety of possibilities, from single rooms to complete houses, delivering a more local and customized experience.

These travel apps and websites may substantially aid you in planning and navigating your trip to Italy. Remember to confirm their availability and compatibility with your device before flying. Embrace the ease of technology to make your Italian experience easier and more fun!

- Italian Cultural References

Italy is a nation rich in culture that has made great contributions to art, literature, music, fashion, and gastronomy. Understanding Italian cultural allusions may expand your awareness of the country's history and enrich your vacation experience. Here is a complete analysis of some famous Italian cultural references:

1. **Renaissance**: Italy is famous as the cradle of the Renaissance, an era of significant cultural and creative accomplishments. Artists like Leonardo da Vinci, Michelangelo, and Raphael made works that continue to inspire and enchant people worldwide.

2. **Ancient Rome**: Italy was once the core of the Roman Empire, and Roman civilization left a lasting imprint on the globe. Historical buildings such as the Colosseum, the Roman Forum, and the Pantheon are reminders of Rome's great past.

3. **Opera**: Italy is famed for its rich opera legacy, with composers like Verdi, Puccini, and Rossini providing timeless compositions. The legendary La Scala in Milan and the Arena di Verona are classic settings for opera performances.

4. **Classical Music**: Italy has produced several significant classical composers, notably Antonio Vivaldi and Giuseppe Tartini. The nation also hosts other music festivals, such as the Puccini Festival in Tuscany and the Salzburg Festival in Austria.

5. **Catholicism**: Italy is largely Catholic, and the Vatican City, an autonomous city-state inside Rome, is the spiritual and administrative center of the Catholic Church. The nation is home to countless great churches, cathedrals, and religious art.

6. **Fashion**: Italy is a worldwide fashion powerhouse, with cities like Milan, Rome, and Florence at the heart of the industry. Italian designers, like Gucci, Prada, Versace, and Armani, have had a significant effect on fashion trends worldwide.

7. **Gastronomy**: Italian food is known internationally for its simplicity, excellent

ingredients, and regional uniqueness. Pasta, pizza, gelato, and espresso are some quintessential Italian gastronomic pleasures. Each area has its distinctive foods and peculiarities.

8. **Wine**: Italy is one of the world's leading wine producers and provides a broad choice of superb wines. Regions like Tuscany, Piedmont, and Veneto are recognized to generate renowned wines such as Chianti, Barolo, and Prosecco.

9. **Football (Soccer)**: Football is loved in Italy, and the nation enjoys a robust football culture. Serie A, the main Italian football league, comprises notable clubs like Juventus, AC Milan, and Inter Milan. The Italian national team has a long history and has won the FIFA World Cup many times.

10. **Fiat and Ferrari**: Italy is famed for its automotive sector. Fiat, based in Turin, is one of the country's largest vehicle manufacturers. Ferrari, famed for its premium sports vehicles, is a globally recognized icon of Italian engineering and design.

11. **Literature**: Italy has a strong literary legacy, with notable writers like Dante Alighieri, Petrarch, and Italo Calvino. Dante's

"Divine Comedy" is a masterwork of global literature, whereas Calvino's works, such as "Invisible Cities," exhibit his inventive storytelling.

12. **Cinema**: Italian cinema has produced significant filmmakers and classic movies. The neorealism movement of the mid-20th century, pioneered by filmmakers like Federico Fellini and Vittorio De Sica, introduced realist and social criticism to the cinema.

13. **Mosaic Art**: Italy is famed for its complex mosaic art, visible in ancient Roman villas, churches, and cathedrals. Ravenna, in particular, is famed for its Byzantine mosaics, particularly those found in the Basilica of San Vitale.

14. **Holidays**: Italy celebrates several cultural and religious holidays throughout the year. The Carnival of Venice, with its spectacular masks and costumes, and the Palio di Siena, a medieval horse race, are among the country's most recognized festivals.

Understanding these cultural allusions will offer you a broader perspective into Italy's history, customs, and modern accomplishments. It will enable you to interact with the country's past and experience the richness of Italian culture throughout your stay.

- Online Forums and Communities

In the digital era, online forums and communities have become important venues for connecting with like-minded people, exchanging knowledge, and seeking guidance. Whether you're seeking travel ideas, language exchange partners, or debates about Italian culture, there are various internet forums and groups devoted to Italy. Here's a thorough overview of major web platforms in Italy:

1. TripAdvisor Italy Forum (www.tripadvisor.com/ShowForum-g187768-i2 0-Italy.html): The TripAdvisor Italy Forum is a popular location for tourists seeking advice, suggestions, and travel-related topics. It covers numerous themes such as locations, lodgings, attractions, and transportation.

2. Expat.com Italy Forum (www.expat.com/forum/viewforum.php?id=564): Expat.com provides a forum exclusively devoted to Italy, offering a venue for ex-pats and potential ex-pats to share information and advice regarding living, working, and migrating to Italy.

3. InterNations Italy Community (www.internations.org/italy-expats): InterNations is a worldwide community for expatriates, and its Italy section enables ex-pats in Italy to interact, mingle, and share vital information on life in the country.

4. Italophile Book Reviews Forum (italophilebookreviews.blogspot.com/p/forum.html): The Italophile Book Reviews Forum is a platform for book enthusiasts interested in Italian literature, history, and culture. It gives book suggestions, debates, and author interviews.

5. Italian Language Forum (www.italian-language-forum.com): This forum is devoted to studying the Italian language. It provides tools, language exercises, and a forum for language learners to ask questions, practice, and participate in debates connected to the Italian language and culture.

6. Italy Magazine Forum (www.italymagazine.com/forums): Italy Magazine offers an active community forum where members may debate all elements of Italian culture, tourism, cuisine, and language. It also gives a place for discussing travel experiences and seeking guidance.

7. Italian Genealogy Forum (www.italiangenealogy.com/forum): If you're interested in researching your Italian heritage, the Italian Genealogy Forum is a valuable resource. It provides information, research recommendations, and a friendly network for anyone discovering their Italian family history.

8. Italy Chronicles Forum (www.italychronicles.com/forum): Italy Chronicles is an English-language online magazine about Italy, and its forum enables readers to debate a variety of issues connected to Italian culture, news, politics, and tourism.

9. Slow Travel Talk Forum (slowtalk.com): Slow Travel is a concept that fosters a deeper and more immersive travel experience. The Slow Travel Talk Forum offers a venue for travelers to exchange their slow travel experiences, suggestions, and insights in Italy.

10. Italiamerica Forum (www.italiamerica.org/id81.htm): The Italiamerica Forum focuses on Italian-American culture and tradition. It provides a platform for debates concerning Italian-American history, ancestry, customs, and links between Italy and the United States.

These online forums and groups provide an important opportunity to interact with individuals who share your interests in Italy, whether it's travel, language, culture, or ancestry. They offer a friendly and instructive atmosphere for sharing experiences, obtaining assistance, and building a feeling of community.

CONCLUSION

- Final Tips and Recommendations

As you prepare for your vacation to Italy, here are some last suggestions and advice to guarantee a smooth and pleasurable experience:

1. **Plan**: Italy is a popular tourist destination, therefore it's important to plan your vacation. Research the places you wish to see, make reservations for popular locations, and check for any special events or holidays that may alter your schedule.

2. **Respect the Culture**: Italians take pride in their culture and customs. Familiarize oneself with basic Italian manners, such as greeting people with "Buongiorno" (good morning) or "Buona sera" (good evening), and adopting a more modest clothing code, particularly while visiting religious places.

3. **Learn Basic Italian words**: While many Italians understand English, knowing a few basic Italian words may go a long way in forging relationships and showing respect. Practice words like "Grazie" (thank you), "per favor" (please), and "scusi" (pardon me).

4. **Be Mindful of Pickpockets**: Like at any tourist site, be mindful of Pickpockets, especially around busy places. Keep your possessions tight, avoid flaunting precious goods, and consider utilizing a money belt or a lockable bag to protect your valuables.

5. **Try Local Food**: Italian food is recognized internationally, and each area has its specialties. Embrace the gastronomic joys of Italy by sampling genuine cuisine, visiting local markets, and touring classic trattorias and gelaterias.

6. **Use Public Transit**: Italy boasts an effective public transit system, including trains and buses. Opt for public transit while touring cities to minimize traffic and parking issues. Consider acquiring a regional transit pass or utilizing applications like Moovit or Google Maps for route planning.

7. **Verify Train Tickets**: If you're going by train, remember to verify your ticket using the yellow machines at the station before boarding. Failure to do so may result in a fine.

8. **Explore Beyond the Major Cities**: While Rome, Florence, and Venice are famous destinations, Italy offers many hidden beauties worth visiting. Consider visiting smaller cities

and locations like Cinque Terre, Siena, Puglia, or the Amalfi Coast for a more genuine and off-the-beaten-path experience.

9. **Take Leisure to Relax**: Italians appreciate their "dolce far niente" (sweet doing nothing) leisure. Embrace Italian culture by taking leisurely walks, sipping a cappuccino at a local café, and embracing moments of relaxation throughout your stay

10. **Stay Flexible**: While it's helpful to have a plan, also be open to unexpected discoveries and possibilities. Allow yourself to roam the picturesque neighborhoods, mingle with people, and accept the serendipity that may make your vacation even more unforgettable.

Remember, Italy provides a multitude of cultural, historical, and gastronomic adventures. Embrace the beauty of the nation, immerse yourself in its rich legacy, and make amazing memories during your stay in Italy. Buon Viaggio! (Have a wonderful trip!)

- Your Next Adventure Awaits!

Italy, a nation of magnificent scenery, rich history, lively culture, and exquisite food, invites people from across the globe. From the ancient ruins of Rome to the gorgeous canals of Venice and the rolling hills of Tuscany, Italy offers a broad assortment of experiences that will leave you enthralled. Here's a detailed resource to inspire your next journey in Italy:

1. **Explore Rome**: Begin your Italian vacation in the eternal city of Rome. Marvel at classic sites such as the Colosseum, the Roman Forum, and the Pantheon. Discover the Vatican City, home of St. Peter's Basilica and the Sistine Chapel, where you may view Michelangelo's masterpiece.

2. **Wander Through Florence**: Immerse yourself in the magnificent treasures of Florence, the cradle of the Renaissance. Visit the Uffizi Gallery to view paintings by Botticelli, Leonardo da Vinci, and Michelangelo. Admire the majestic Duomo and discover the charming alleyways of the Oltrarno area.

3. **Experience the Romance of Venice**: Lose yourself in the picturesque city of Venice, noted for its twisting canals and stunning architecture. Take a gondola ride down the Grand Canal, visit St. Mark's Square and the Doge's Palace, and get lost in the lovely streets of this unique city.

4. **Discover the Beauty of Tuscany**: Indulge in the rustic appeal of Tuscany, with its rolling hills, vineyards, and historic villages. Visit the enchanting city of Siena, experience the Renaissance magnificence of Florence's surroundings, and sample the world-famous wines of the Chianti area.

5. **Experience the Amalfi Coast**: Embark on a tour through the magnificent Amalfi Coast, with its towering cliffs, pastel-colored towns, and blue seas. Explore the lovely hamlet of Positano, explore the ancient ruins of Pompeii, and take in the breathtaking views from Ravello.

6. **Marvel at the Cinque Terre**: Discover the lovely seaside towns of the Cinque Terre, a UNESCO World Heritage site. Hike along the picturesque paths, see the colorful fishing towns, and indulge in delicious seafood and local wines.

7. **Unwind in Sicily**: Escape to the island of Sicily, where ancient Greek temples, lovely seaside villages, and wonderful food await. Explore the Valley of the Temples in Agrigento, explore the bustling marketplaces of Palermo,

and ascend Mount Etna, Europe's highest active volcano.

8. **Delight in the Lakes Area**: Experience the peacefulness of Italy's lakes area, including Lake Como, Lake Garda, and Lake Maggiore. Relax at magnificent homes, take boat trips, and enjoy the stunning views that have charmed travelers for decades.

9. **Indulge in Italian Cuisine**: Italy is a food lover's heaven, providing a delectable choice of regional delicacies and local specialties. Sample traditional Neapolitan pizza in Naples, indulge in gelato in Florence, and relish fresh seafood on the coast. Don't forget to complement your meals with wonderful Italian wines.

10. **Embrace Italian Festivals**: Throughout the year, Italy offers exciting festivals and events that reflect its traditions and culture. Witness the ancient Palio di Siena horse race, enjoy Carnevale in Venice, or join the festivities of the Verona Opera Festival.

Italy's stunning beauty, rich history, and warm friendliness await your next journey. Whether you're exploring ancient ruins, enjoying gastronomic pleasures, or bathing in the natural magnificence, Italy provides a voyage of a lifetime. So pack your bags, immerse yourself in la dolce vita, and let your next journey

unravel in the wonderful nation of Italy!

BONUS: Quick Reference Guides

- Italian Phrases and Expressions

Learning some important Italian words and expressions will substantially improve your trip experience in Italy. It demonstrates respect for the local culture, helps you negotiate everyday encounters, and enables you to engage with people on a more personal level. Here is a thorough collection of basic Italian phrases and expressions:

1. **Basic Greetings**:

- Ciao! (Hello!/Goodbye!) - This adaptable welcome works in both official and casual contexts.

- Buongiorno! (Good morning!/Good day!) - Used till mid-afternoon as a welcome.

- Buonasera! (Good evening!) - Used as a welcome from late afternoon onwards.

- Arrivederci! (Goodbye!) - Used while parting ways.

- Grazie! (Thank you!) - Expresses thanks.

- Prego! (You're welcome!/Please!) - Used to answer "thank you" or while providing something.

2. Polite Expressions:

- Per favore (Please) - Used while making a courteous request.

- Scusa/Scusami (Excuse me/I'm sorry) - Used to catch someone's attention or apologize.

- Mi scusi (Excuse me/Sorry) - Formal variant of "scuba/scams."

- Permesso (May I come in?) - Used when asking permission to enter an area.

3. Introductions and Basic Conversations:

- Come ti chiami? (What's your name?)
- Mi chiamo... (My name is...)
- Piacere di concerti. (Nice to meet you.)
- Parla inglese? (Do you speak English?)
- Non Capisco. (I don't understand.)
- Parla più lentamente, per favore. (Speak more slowly, please.)
- Mi scuso, non parlo bene l'italiano. (I'm sorry, I don't speak Italian well.)

4. Asking for Help and Directions:

- Mi può aiutare? (Can you assist me?)
- Dove si trova...? (Where is...?)
- Scusi, dove posso trovare un ristorante? (Excuse me, where can I locate a restaurant?)
- A sinister (to the left) / A destra (to the right)
- Useful for providing or following instructions.
- È lontano? (Is it far?)

5. **Ordering Food and Drinks**: - Vorrei... (I would like...)

   - Il menù, per favore. (The menu, please.)

   - Mi può consigliare un piatto tipico? (Can you suggest a typical dish?)

   - Un caffè, per favore. (A coffee, please.)

   - Un bicchiere di vino rosso/Bianco, per favore. (A glass of red/white wine, please.)

6. **Numbers and Money**:

- Uno, due, tre... (One, two, three...)

   - Quanto costa? (How much does it cost?)

   - Posso pagare con la carta di credito? (Can I pay with a credit card?)

7. **Common Expressions**:

   - Mi piace! (I like it!)

   - Mi dispiace. (I'm sorry.)

   - Molto bene! (Very excellent!)

   - Va bene. (That's fine/Okay.)

   - Non Importa. (It doesn't matter.)

Remember, repetition and pronunciation are crucial to learning these phrases. Italians admire your attempt to speak their language, even if you make errors. So, embrace the language, mingle with the people, and make the most of your Italian vacation!

Conversion Tables

CURRENCY	MEASUREMENTS
DOLLAR	
EURO	
GBP	
AUD	
CAD	

- Emergency Contacts and Useful Numbers

When traveling or staying in Italy, it's crucial to be aware of the emergency contact numbers and utilize numbers that may aid you in different scenarios. Whether you want quick medical treatment, need to report a crime, or seek help from government authorities, having access to these numbers may be important. Here is a full list of emergency contacts and handy numbers in Italy:

1. **Emergency Services**:
   - Emergency (General): 112
   - Police: 113
   - Carabinieri (Military Police): 112 or 113
   - Ambulance/Emergency Medical Services: 118
   - Fire Brigade: 115
   - Coast Guard: 1530
   - Mountain Rescue: 118

2. **Medical Services**:
   - First Aid and Non-emergency Medical Services: 118
   - Poison Control Center: 800 858585
   - Anti-Poison Information Centre (Milan): 02 6610 3742

3. **Useful Numbers**:
   - Tourist Helpline (Multilingual): 892021

- Directory Assistance: 12 or 1240

- Roadside Assistance: 803.116

- Lost or Stolen Credit Cards: Contact your bank's emergency hotline or the international helpline indicated on your credit card.

4. **Government and Administrative Services**: - Italian Embassy/Consulate: Contact the embassy or consulate of your home country in Italy for their unique contact details.

- Immigration Office: Contact the local Questura (Police Headquarters) or the local Prefettura (Prefecture) for immigration-related problems.

- Municipal Police: The number might vary by city, so verify with the local authorities or look for the appropriate number online.

5. **Transport and Travel Services**:

- Road Traffic Information: 1518

- Train Information: 892021

- Lost and Found (Public Transportation): Contact the appropriate local transit authority or visit their website for information on lost goods.

6. **Legal Assistance**: - Legal Emergency Hotline: 803 193

7. **Child and Family Support**:

- Child Helpline: 114

- National Anti-Violence Hotline: 1522

It's crucial to remember that although these numbers are usually relevant across Italy, there can be some regional differences or extra local emergency contacts particular to certain localities. It's good to investigate and have access to local emergency numbers if you intend to visit or dwell in a given location.

It's also important to have a basic comprehension of the Italian language, particularly when calling emergency services, since the operators may have poor English competence. If required, attempt to locate a translator or someone who can aid you in conveying your issue properly.

Remember to use these emergency contacts responsibly and only for actual emergencies or circumstances that demand a quick response.

Printed in Great Britain
by Amazon

39333137R00155